THE CAMBRIDGE – TILBURG
LAW LECTURES

THE CAMBRIDGE-TILBURG LAW LECTURES

SECOND SERIES 1979

Editors: Dr B.S. Markesinis and Mr J.H.M. Willems

The Judicial Protection of Fundamental Rights under English Law

by

J. A. JOLOWICZ

M.A., Professor of Comparative Law in the University of Cambridge, Fellow and Dean of Trinity College, Bencher of Gray's Inn.

The Infiltration of Equity into English Commercial Law

by

G. JONES

M.A., LL.D., Downing Professor of the Laws of England in the University of Cambridge, Fellow of Trinity College, Barrister at Law of Lincoln's Inn.

1980

Springer Science+Business Media, B.V.

The Cambridge – Tilburg Law Lectures

1978: First Series

J.A. Weir:	Compensation for personal injuries and death: Recent proposals for reform
D.G.T. Williams:	The accountability of the police: Two studies

Library of Congress Catalog Card Number: 80 – 36896

ISBN 978-90-268-1166-1 ISBN 978-94-017-4414-0 (eBook)
DOI 10.1007/978-94-017-4414-0

Originally published by Kluwer Academic Publishers in 1980.

THE CAMBRIDGE – TILBURG LAW LECTURES

Organising Committee

Cambridge	*Tilburg*
Prof. C.J. Hamson, Q.C., LL.M.	Prof. Mr J. E. J. Th. Deelen
Prof. Gareth Jones, M.A., LL.D.	Prof. Mr H. J. M. Jeukens
Prof. J. A. Jolowicz, M.A.	Prof. Mr H. C. F. Schoordijk
D. G. T. Williams, M.A. LL.B.	Prof. Mr F. H. van der Burg
J. A. Weir, M.A.	Prof. Mr B. S. Frenkel

Directors of Studies

B. S. Markesinis, D. Iur., M.A., Ph.D. — Mr J. H. M. Willems

FOREWORD

The year 1978 marked the thirtieth anniversary of Professor C. J. Hamson's 'Summer course for foreign lawyers' and of his untiring efforts not only to introduce the civil lawyer to the mysteries of the Common law but also to bring closer together lawyers from both sides of the Channel. The same year saw the beginning of the 'Cambridge-Tilburg Law Lectures' which developed indirectly from the 'Summer course' and which seek to achieve similar aims by different methods.

The idea of inviting two Cambridge scholars to assist their Dutch colleagues in the teaching of the Common law as a regular option for undergraduate studies is novel and, to judge from first reactions, has so far been successful. The immediate objects are to achieve closer links between lawyer and Civil lawyer; to encourage the further systematic teaching of the Common law; and to produce a series of lectures, two of which will be published annually in the hope that they may be of interest to a wider public.

The realisation of this idea became possible thanks to the generosity of the Tilburg Law Faculty and the impressive energy, enthusiasm and hospitality of its members. To name all who in divers ways contributed to the realisation of this scheme is, unfortunately, impossible but the names of Professor Jeukens, Schoordijk and Deelen demand special attention. On the Cambridge side the project was extremely fortunate to gain the early support of Professor Gareth Jones, Professor Tony Jolowicz, Mr. David Williams and Mr. Tony Weir.

The second series of the Cambridge-Tilburg Law Lectures were delivered in Tilburg in March 1979 by Professor J. A. Jolowicz and Professor Gareth Jones and once again are published by the Tilburg Law Faculty in association with Kluwer Publishers.

B. S. Markesinis J. H. M. Willems

TABLE OF CONTENTS

THE JUDICIAL PROTECTION OF FUNDAMENTAL RIGHTS UNDER ENGLISH LAW

by

J. A. Jolowicz

The Judicial Protection of Fundamental Rights under English Law

Prefatory observation

This paper, which is based on a course of lectures delivered in Tilburg in March 1979, represents the attempt of a 'private' lawyer to explain some aspects of English law as they relate to 'fundamental rights.' To the professing 'public' lawyer the approach adopted and, in particular, the reduction to three only in the number of 'rights' specifically discussed, may seem strange. An English 'public' lawyer would, however, probably agree that the formal distinction between 'public' and 'private' law has been of little importance in England save for academic purposes and he would also agree, at least if pressed, that the casuistical nature of English law renders somewhat artificial and unhistorical the attempt to expound it as a system of 'rights.' His preconceptions and the inarticulate premises that inform his approach to a legal subject are more likely than those of the 'private' lawyer to lead him into a treatment of 'fundamental rights' which takes as its starting point a number of 'Rights' and he will, very properly, draw attention to the undoubted importance in the modern world of the various Declarations of Rights which have legal force in other national legal systems and in international or supra-national law. As will appear, however, no such Declaration has as yet the force of law in England, and it is one of the purposes of this paper to convey an impression of the style and methods of English law to readers trained in a different system: it is not in its own right an exercise in comparative law which must take as its starting point something which is common to more than one legal system. It is not, therefore, altogether a disadvantage that this paper should adopt a stance which may be unfamiliar to its readers provided, of course, that it does not actually mislead. English law is, and for centuries has been, concerned principally with litigation and what happens in the courts rather than with great statements of constitutional principle which tend to be seen either as a means for reaching particular decisions or as belonging more to politics than to law. The 'public' lawyer more than the 'private' lawyer seeks to escape from this idea of 'law', and it is for this reason as much as for any other that it is hoped that a 'private' lawyer's account of the protection of 'fundamental rights' which says little about such rights is, at least for present purposes, a less bizarre undertaking than it might at first sight appear to be.

Part I
Introductory

The United Kingdom, of which England forms a part, has no written constitution and there are no codes. There is, of course, a great volume of legislation, but the decisions of the courts are recognised as sources of law which are, in their own right and subject to the rules for the operation of the doctrine of precedent, binding authorities for the decision of subsequent cases. There is no legislative statement of constitutionally protected 'rights', there is not even much legislative statement of general principle such as is found in a continental code, and it is still rare – it was formerly almost unknown – for legal reasoning to take as its starting point the 'right' of an individual with a view to deciding whether or not that 'right' has been infringed.[1] Speaking generally, English law, being an amalgam of legislation and case law, is too casuistical for that. If, therefore, we speak of 'fundamental' or 'human' rights in relation to English law, the catalogue of 'rights' with which we start must be taken from outside the formal statements of the law itself: we are compelled to refer either to some international declaration of Human Rights or to a list of such 'rights' which we compose for ourselves *a priori*. This statement calls for explanation and expansion from several points of view.

1. REMEDIES PRECEDE RIGHTS

During the early formative period of the English common law the King's courts – the only centralised jurisdiction in the country – were neither in practice nor in theory courts of universal competence. Originally they were competent only in cases of concern to the King, and over the centuries they gradually enlarged their competence at the expense of the other jurisdictions through the development and expansion of 'remedies', that is of procedures whereby a person could bring before the court a specific complaint of a wrong done to him in respect of which he sought redress. By the time of the great reforms of the nineteenth century the Royal courts had come to possess a competence

1. This is not, of course, to say that the word 'right' is not a word regularly used, even by lawyers, and the increasing use of the word in a 'non-Hohfeldian' sense – social 'rights', the 'right to strike' and so on – is beginning to have an effect on the law itself. For a case in which a legal conclusion was reached by Lord Denning M.R. on the basis that there is a 'right to strike', see *Morgan* v. *Fry* (1968) 2 Q.B. 710, 725.

which was in practice universal, but that universality came rather from the overall scope of the various different 'remedies' than from a general principle of theoretical validity. So far as the non-criminal law is concerned – and it must be borne in mind that England does not have and never has had a distinct 'administrative' jurisdiction – those remedies consisted of the so-called 'forms of action' for civil cases and the 'prerogative writs' whereby the decisions of certain 'inferior' jurisdictions could be challenged before the court. It was essential for the intending complainant to bring his case within one of these 'remedies', and the first question that the lawyer had to consider on behalf of his client was not 'Has my client a right?' but 'Has he a remedy?'. So rigid was this system until the reforms of the last century that selection of the wrong remedy for the plaintiff's case was fatal: an action started in the wrong form would be dismissed without any consideration of the substantive merits of the plaintiff's case.[2]

During the nineteenth century the forms of action as such were abolished,[3] and much more recently the 'prerogative writs' have been greatly simplified from the procedural point of view and have been brought together under the single heading of 'application for judicial review.'[4] It is no longer possible for an action to fail merely because it was started in the wrong form. This does not mean, however, that the casuistical character of English law and its emphasis on remedies rather than on rights has disappeared. It is true that now, more than a century after the abolition of the forms of action, a judge's reasoning may occasionally take as its starting point the plaintiff's right and deduce that a remedy is available for its infringement, but that is still regarded as a little eccentric. So far as systematisation of the law and the statement of general principle are concerned – and both are to be found today in the judgments of the courts as well as in the writings of legal scholars – attention is generally concentrated on the circumstances in which a judicial remedy is available to a complainant, that is on 'wrongs' rather than on 'rights.' And, though a 'wrong' may be no more than a correlative of a 'right', this means that an analysis and account of the 'rights' that are protected by English law, whether 'fundamental' or not, still appears to most English lawyers to involve a reversal of his customary mode of thought.[5]

2. See David & Brierly *Major Legal Systems in the World today*, 2nd ed., 294.

3. This was not achieved at one stroke. The most important change was to allow more than one form of action to be pleaded in a single case: Common Law Procedure Act 1852.

4. Rules of the Supreme Court, 0.53, introduced in 1977.

5. The English mode of thought is epitomised in the definition given by Diplock L.J. to 'cause of action' in *Letang* v. *Cooper* (1965) 1 Q.B. 232, 242-243. 'A cause of action is simply a factual situation the existence of which entitles one person to obtain from the courts a remedy against another person'.

2. THE EUROPEAN CONVENTION FOR THE PROTECTION OF HUMAN RIGHTS AND FUNDAMENTAL FREEDOMS

The United Kingdom is a party to the United Nations' Universal Declaration of Human Rights and also to the European Convention. The latter provides machinery for its own enforcement through the Commission and the Court at Strasbourg; since 1966 the United Kingdom has accepted the right of individual petition to Strasbourg for which the Convention provides. The Convention does, of course, take as its starting point a declaration of the rights which it is sought to protect and it might be argued, therefore, that adherence to the Convention has introduced into English law a catalogue of rights having the force of law.[6]

It is true that at the international level the United Kingdom, as a party to the Convention, must accept the legal validity of the rights which it contains, but it does not follow that the same is true for English domestic law with which alone this paper is concerned. On the contrary, it is well established that the provisions of a Treaty – and the Convention is a Treaty – become part of English law only if Parliament passes legislation to that effect, and no 'enabling' Act giving the force of law in England to the Convention has yet been passed.

On the face of things, therefore, the European Convention is no more relevant to the law and its administration in the English courts today than it was before the United Kingdom became a party to it. This, as recent developments have tended to show, would actually be an overstatement for there are now numerous references to the Convention to be found in English cases, but it is still maintained that the Convention as such forms no part of English law. The use made by the judges of the Convention has been little if anything more than as a guide to the interpretation of unclear or ambiguous legislation; on the assumption that the task of a court called upon to interpret an Act of Parliament is, first and foremost, to discover the intention of Parliament, it is proper for the court to presume in a case of doubt that Parliament did not intend to disregard the international obligations of the United Kingdom, and the Convention shows, within its sphere of operation, what those obligations are.[7] Occasionally, it is true, the attempt has been made to give greater effect than that to the provisions of the Convention,[8] but so far they have not succeeded; and it has

6. See Mann, 'Britain's Bill of Rights' (1978) 94 L.Q.R. 512.
7. See e.g. *R.* v. *Miah* (1974) 1 W.L.R. 683, *R.* v. *Home Secretary, ex p. Bhajan Singh* (1976) Q.B. 198; *R.* v. *Chief Immigration Officer, ex p. Bibi* (1976) 1 W.L.R. 979; *Ahmad* v. *Inner London Education Authority* (1978) Q.B. 36.
8. E.g. the dissenting judgment of Scarman L.J. in *Ahmad* v. *Inner London Education Authority, supra*.

recently been held that where the question before the court does not depend on the interpretation of legislation, then the Convention has no bearing on the solution to be adopted by the court.[9]

In the light of this, it is necessary to conclude that the rights set out in the Convention cannot be regarded as a 'Bill of Rights' contained within English law, but in any case such a 'Bill of Rights' would not easily be accommodated into the English style of administering justice. The question whether a 'Bill of Rights' in the form of the Convention or in some other form could usefully be enacted is considered briefly later in this paper, but the contemporary reaction of English judges to the kind of broad statement of principle it contains is clearly brought out in the words of Lord Denning M.R. in a case decided in 1978. It was Lord Denning who was influential in persuading the courts to look at the Convention, and in the case itself he actually said that 'we shall always have regard to it. We will do our best to see that our decisions are in conformity with it. But', he continued, 'it is drawn in such vague terms that it can be used for all sorts of unreasonable claims and provoke all sorts of litigation. As so often happens with high sounding principles, they have to be brought down to earth. They have to be applied in a work-a-day world.' And then, coming to the facts of the case, in which a Muslim school-teacher had sought to rely on Article 9 of the Convention in a dispute with his employers, Lord Denning observed tartly, 'I see nothing in the European Convention to give Mr. Ahmad any right to manifest his religion on Friday afternoons in derogation of his contract of employment: and certainly not on full pay.'[10]

3. THE CASUISTICAL CHARACTER OF THE LAW

For the purposes of the present exposition, this topic must be considered under two separate headings, first the fact that English law is a case law system and secondly the importance of decisions to the actual operation of law within society.

A. When it is said that the English legal system is a case-law system, what is meant, primarily, is that the English system accords the formal status of sources of law to the decisions of the courts. The actual working of the case-law system is complex and cannot be examined here, but one of its essential features is that every court is 'bound' by the decisions of those superior to itself in the judicial hierarchy, and that, though slightly more controversially, the Court of Appeal is bound by its own decisions[11]; indeed, it is only since 1966 that the

9. *Malone* v. *Metropolitan Police Commissioner* (1979) Ch. 344.
10. *Ahmad* v. *Inner London Education Authority*, *supra*.
11. See *Davis* v. *Johnson* (1979) A.C. 264.

House of Lords has become free of the fetters of it own precedents.[12] Of course a previous decision is only 'binding' in circumstances to which it applies, which gives rise to the important technique of 'distinguishing' one case from another, and of course the judges themselves, in explaining their own decisions, analyse, synthesise and rationalise the precedent decisions in such a way as to enunciate principles of law: not many lawyers in common law countries would accept as completely accurate Jerome Frank's statement that law is 'actual specific past *decisions* and guesses as to actual specific future decisions.'[13] Nevertheless the emphasis on actual decisions inherent in a case-law system focuses attention much more closely than in a 'civil law' system on the judicial process itself: though 'the law' is more than an amalgam of decisions even in areas relatively untouched by legislation, almost all English lawyers would regard the idea of law as something apart from the decisions of the courts as being too far removed from reality to be of interest to any but the most abstract of legal theorists.

B. There are many factors other than the law which influence behaviour in society, and it cannot be seriously maintained even that the law is the only one which prevents a person from acting in his own selfish interest to the detriment of others. This needs no elaboration. But the specific contribution of the law to societal control is through the specific decision, actual or hypothetical, which is related to specific circumstances. These decisions are not exclusively the decisions of the courts themselves, for innumerable officials from the highest to the lowest daily make decisions which are not essentially different from those made by the courts: the Customs Officer who charges me duty on my tobacco or the police officer who stops me for speeding bases his action on his application of the law to the facts, and that is what judges do too. Even more significant, however, are the decisions which we make for ourselves, with or without professional advice, about our own actions, actual or contemplated, if the law enters into our calculations at all. What we look for for ourselves, or what we want from our legal advisers, is not the statement of a general principle but the actual conclusion, the particular legal result, that follows from the application of the law to the facts which we have in mind. The law does not exist for lawyers but for all who live under it, and when a man asks 'What is the law about this?' what he means, unless his enquiry is academic, is 'What would a court decide if it had these facts before it?'

It is not intended to deny that statements of legal principle may sometimes affect behaviour in society otherwise than through decisions, actual or hypothetical. A statement of legal principle may, for example,

12. *Practice Statement (Judicial Precedent)* (1966) 1 W.L.R. 1234.
13. Frank, *Law and the Modern Mind*, 47.

have an important educational effect. But in so far as it does so operate, the mechanism of its operation is not significantly different from that of other educational factors influencing behaviour such as the prevailing morality or the demands of religion. The judicial decision is the archetype of what the law *does* in society, and the special contribution of the law to society, including the protection of 'fundamental' rights, stems from that.[14]

Even if English law were not essentially court-orientated in its approach, therefore, an examination of the legal protection of fundamental rights in England could not fail to concentrate on the decisions of the courts, but the absence of a formal statement of those rights in legislative form renders a more abstract or theoretical approach impossible. If the existence and nature of a right can only be deduced from the remedies available to the victims of a 'wrong', it follows that a 'right', so far as the law is concerned, is co-extensive with its protection through the action of the law, that is with the availability of a legal remedy in the courts. We may say that a man has certain rights, and we commonly do say just that, but if by our statement we mean more than that in certain circumstances he can secure redress from another through the medium of judicial decision, then we are using the word 'right' in a sense that involves reference to something outside the prevailing positive law of the society in which we live. Provided, however, that this is borne in mind, there is no reason why an account of the English law should not take as its starting point one or more 'rights' broadly expressed and chosen *a priori*, and that is the approach that will be adopted in relation to the specific 'rights', taken for the purpose of illustration, in the following Part of this paper.[15]

14. For a fuller statement of this see Jolowicz, 'The Case for Applied Comparative Law' in Cappelletti (ed.) *New Perspectives for a Common Law of Europe*, 237, 239-243.
15. For an account by the author of 'fundamental rights' in civil litigation in England, see his contribution to Cappelletti and Tallon (ed.), *Fundamental Guarantees of the Parties in Civil Litigation*, 121.

Part II
Some Particular Rights

1. THE RIGHT OF ACCESS TO THE COURTS

If it is correct that the judicial decision is the archetype of what the law does in society, and if it is also correct that, so far as the law itself is concerned, a 'right' is coextensive with its judicial protection, then it follows that a 'rights-based' account of any part of the law must consider, first and foremost, the 'right of access to the courts.' Two main aspects of this fall to be discussed, namely, the competence of the courts to receive complaints from persons whose interests are adversely affected by the actions of others – what may be called the 'legal right of access' – and the methods employed to ensure, so far as possible, that exercise of that 'legal right of access' is not in practice the exclusive privilege of those sufficiently endowed, financially and otherwise, to make use of it from their own resources. In addition, however, it is convenient to consider under this head a problem of increasing importance in modern conditions, namely, the right, if any, of individuals or groups to challenge before the courts the legality of the actions of others not on the ground of their own private interest but on the ground of the general or group interest as a whole.

A. The Legal Right of Access to the Courts

The absence of a written constitution and thus of any provision such as that in the German Constitution that 'Everyone has the right to be heard before the court'[16] does, admittedly, mean that the court itself can decline to hear a complaint even from a person who claims to have suffered some harm at the defendant's hands: the court will not, for example, consider an action brought by a University student alleging that his examiners were negligent in reaching the decision that he had failed his examinations.[17] As a general rule, however, there is no obstacle in the way of the person who wishes to bring an ordinary civil action and, as will appear, the civil action, especially the action based on tort, is one of the principal vehicles for the protection of certain 'fundamental' rights such as the right to personal liberty. Formerly, it is true, no action in tort could be brought against the Crown, but that

16. Constitution of the Federal Republic of Germany (G.G.), art. 103 § 1.
17. *Thorne* v. *University of London* (1966) 2 Q.B. 237.

consequence of the ancient maxim 'the King can do no wrong' was finally removed by the Crown Proceedings Act 1947.

The most important matter for consideration here relates to the possibility of challenging before the court the actions and, more particularly, the decisions of persons or bodies entrusted with discretionary powers when those actions or decisions adversely affect the interests of individuals. The subject is generally discussed today under the title 'Judicial Review of Administrative Action'[18] and is regarded as belonging to 'Administrative Law', but it is no longer possible to keep it strictly within those bounds, partly because there is no separate administrative jurisdiction and partly because so many non-statutory bodies such as Trade Unions and professional organisations today have powers over the individual, especially in connection with his employment, that are at least as great as those possessed by governmental authorities. It is true that the special remedies now grouped together as 'judicial review'[19] are, generally speaking, available only against bodies exercising powers under a statute, but the civil action is capable of performing an analogous purpose when used against non-statutory bodies, and as a result the substantive law concerning judicial review of the decisions of statutory bodies can come to apply equally to the more important non-statutory bodies as well.

As the author of this paper ventured to say on a different occasion,[20] 'in a modern state it is a question of extreme difficulty to find the correct balance between the right of the citizen to have his grievance, whatever it may be, considered by a court of law, and the proper functioning of governmental and other decision-making bodies whose task would become almost impossible if every decision ever made were susceptible to challenge before the court.' English law provides no legislative criteria for the maintenance of this balance, preferring to leave the matter ostensibly to special legislation covering each type of case, but some general ideas have been developed by the courts. One such idea is that of 'natural justice' – a phrase which has acquired a technical meaning in English law and indicates broadly no more than procedural fairness – and the courts will nullify or declare void decisions reached in violation of the rules of 'natural justice', provided that the decision-maker is required to observe those rules: it is accepted that some decision-makers such as, for example, the traffic policeman who decides to stop one line of traffic in favour of another or the committee of a small social club which decides that a person shall or shall not be admitted to membership are not required to do so. The question whether a decision

18. See, in particular, de Smith, *Judicial Review of Administrative Action*; Wade, *Administrative Law*.
19. R.S.C.,O.53, *ante*, Part I,1.
20. *Loc. cit. supra*, n. 15, at p. 151.

is open to judicial review on the ground of breach of the rules of 'natural justice' or on some other ground can, however, give rise to difficulty where a discretionary power is conferred by very broad statutory language, language which may even, in some cases, be accompanied by a statement to the effect that the decision in question may not be challenged before a court of law at all. It is in relation to statutory provisions of this kind that the most significant developments have occurred during the last two decades, and the outcome has been substantially to enlarge the citizen's legal right of access to the court.

During the nineteenth century, it appears, the courts were by no means unwilling to receive complaints about the decisions of statutory bodies and to control their legality.[21] During the first part of the present century, however, the tendency of the courts was to adopt a literal approach to the interpretation of the relevant legislation, and this inevitably had the consequence of exempting the decisions of many kinds of body from judicial review.[22] In the notorious case of *Liversidge* v. *Anderson,*[23] which was decided during the Second World War, for example, the House of Lords held, by a majority, that the detention of a person by the Home Secretary could not be challenged even to the extent of requiring the Home Secretary to disclose his reasons. The legislation empowered him to make a detention order if he had 'reasonable cause to believe' a person to be of hostile origin or associations, and the House held that the mere certificate from the Home Secretary stating that he had such 'reasonable cause to believe' was a complete answer to the plaintiff's action – a civil action based on the tort of 'false imprisonment' – whose merits were thus never considered.

Although some indications may be found in earlier cases, it is probably the decision of the House of Lords in 1964,[24] in an action brought by a Chief Constable to challenge the decision of the Police Authority dismissing him from his office, that marks the shift away from literal interpretation and towards enhancement of the right of access to the courts: notwithstanding the absence of express limits to the Police Authority's powers, the Chief Constable's dismissal was annulled because he had not been given adequate details of the charges against him and thus had not had a proper opportunity to defend himself: one of the basic rules of 'natural justice' had been disregarded. Since then there have been numerous cases admitting challenges to discretionary

21. E.g. *Cooper* v. *Wandsworth Board of Works* (1863) 14 C.B.(N.S.) 180.
22. For two rather different cases see *Ex p. Venicoff* (1920) 3 K.B. 72 and *R.* v. *Metropolitan Police Commissioner* (1953) 1 W.L.R. 1150.
23. (1942) A.C. 206.
24. *Ridge* v. *Baldwin* (1964) A.C. 40. See also Tribunals and Enquiries Act 1971, ss. 13, 14, replacing earlier legislation and in particular the Tribunals and Enquiries Act 1958, s. 11.

decisions, and in 1977 the House of Lords reached a decision difficult to reconcile with *Liversidge* v. *Anderson* in terms of general principle: the decision of a Minister was annulled for lack of grounds even though the statutory words only required that the Minister himself should be 'satisfied' that grounds for making the order existed.[25] And already in 1969 the House had greatly expanded the possibility of avoiding the effect of words that purported to prevent access to the courts altogether. In *Anisminic Ltd.* v. *Foreign Compensation Commission*[26] the relevant legislation actually provided that 'the determination by the commission of an application made to them ... shall not be called in question in any court of law.' This, it was clear, could not prevent the court from declaring void a determination that the commission had no competence or 'jurisdiction' to make, but the law has for long recognised a distinction between a decision which is simply incorrect as a matter of law and a decision which the decision-maker had no jurisdiction to make at all. The distinction is clear in theory but difficult to apply in practice; by its decision in the *Anisminic* case the House of Lords has come very close to holding that no decision making body with limited jurisdiction has jurisdiction to make a decision which is wrong in law – and, of course, only the courts themselves can decide whether or not this has occurred. The right of access to the courts is thus substantially secured.

This result has been achieved largely by the determination of the judges to follow the sentiment of a member of the House of Lords expressed in a case in 1960, when he said that 'it is a principle not by any means to be whittled down that the subject's right of recourse to Her Majesty's courts for the determination of his rights is not to be excluded except by clear words.'[27] Acceptance of Parliamentary supremacy requires acceptance of the fact that Parliament can deny the citizen access to the courts, but, save, perhaps, where national security is at stake,[28] the courts themselves will be most reluctant to hold in any case that it has actually succeeded by its language in doing so. What is more, the supremacy of Parliament notwithstanding, the ultimate decision on access to the court in any given case cannot, in the nature of things, rest with anyone but the court itself. Bearing in mind that, in the words of an English Bishop of the eighteenth century, 'whoever hath an absolute authority to interpret any written or spoken law, it is he who is truly the law-giver to all intents and purposes, and not the

25. *Secretary of State for Education* v. *Metropolitan Borough of Tameside* (1977) A.C. 1014. See also *Laker Airways Ltd.* v. *Department of Trade* (1976) Q.B. 643.
26. (1969) 2 A.C. 147. See also *Padfield* v. *Minister of Agriculture* (1968) A.C. 997. On the *Anisminic* case see Wade, 'Constitutional and Administrative Aspects of the Anisminic Case' (1969) 85 L.Q.R. 198.
27. *Pyx Granite Ltd.* v. *Ministry of Housing* (1960) A.C. 260, 286, per Lord Simonds.
28. *R.* v. *Home Secretary, ex p. Hosenball* (1977) 1 W.L.R. 766.

person who first wrote and spoke them,'[29] it may be concluded that the right of access to the court need be no less well protected in England than it is where a constitutional provision dealing with the matter actually exists.

B. Access in Fact

There is nothing new in the idea that people who are too poor to meet the costs of litigation from their own resources should receive some kind of financial help in certain circumstances, but it was not until comparatively recently that this idea came to be linked with that of the 'fundamental' right of access to the courts. Now, however, the link is generally acknowledged to exist and there have even been, in some jurisdictions, judicial decisions to the effect that a denial of legal aid may amount in itself to a denial of a 'fundamental' right.[30]

In England there is, of course, no possibility that a court may pronounce 'illegal' a denial of legal aid in a given case unless the legal aid authority has misapplied the legislation under which it acts: the legislation itself cannot be challenged and no overt question of 'fundamental' right arises. Even if this were not so, however, since it is obviously the case that no legal aid scheme could possibly be required to ensure that everyone be enabled to litigate any claim he likes without cost to himself, questions of degree immediately arise; and questions of degree do not readily admit of solution in terms of 'fundamental' rights.

For this reason, as well as for considerations of space, it would not be appropriate here to attempt a detailed description of the English system of legal aid. On the other hand, since the provision of 'adequate' legal aid must be considered an essential element in the protection of the right of access to the court, a brief account of the English system, from the point of view of the would-be litigant, is necessary.

The underlying concept of the present legal aid scheme in England is that a person possessed of a worth-while claim or defence who is unable to meet the costs of litigation from his own resources should be put in a position to obtain the services of a solicitor and, if necessary, of a barrister, either at no cost to himself or at such maximum cost as he can reasonably afford. The Legal Aid Act 1949,[31] which brought into

29. Bishop Hoadly, *Sermon Preached before the King*, 1717. These words so impressed Gray, *The Nature and Sources of Law*, that he quotes them three times (pp. 100, 120, 164) in support of his view that 'the law of the State ... is composed of the rules which the courts ... lay down for the determination of legal rights and duties': *op. cit.* p. 82.

30. See e.g. the recent decision of the European Court of Human Rights in *Airey* v. *Republic of Ireland*, 9th October 1979, Council of Europe Press Release No. C(79) 31.

31. Now replaced by the Legal Aid Act 1974. The most convenient and up to date source of information is the Report of the Royal Commission on Legal Services (Cmnd. 7648) published in October 1979.

operation the system which, subject to modifications, continues to exist, therefore set up a 'Legal Aid Fund', mainly financed out of public money, from which lawyers' fees and other costs may be met. The Fund itself and the administration of the legal aid scheme is not entrusted to a Government Department but to the Law Society, which is the solicitors' professional organisation, and it is a central feature of the scheme that the grant of legal aid in a given case shall not be dependent or the discretion of any Government official.

Broadly speaking every applicant for legal aid must satisfy two conditions. In the first place his 'disposable' income and capital must not exceed certain maxima, and in the second place a committee of lawyers must be satisfied that his proposed claim or defence is such that a litigant capable of paying the costs himself would be well advised to pursue it in the courts. If he satisfies both conditions the applicant for legal aid will receive a 'legal aid certificate' which will indicate either that he need pay nothing towards the costs himself or, if his income or capital exceeds a certain amount, that he need pay no more than a stated maximum amount. The costs which would, were he not assisted, fall upon him at the end of the litigation are then met from the Legal Aid Fund.

Armed with his legal aid certificate, the would-be litigant is able, without fear of the financial consequences, to instruct the lawyers of his choice. It is true that a small number of lawyers will not accept legal aid work, but the great majority of practitioners is willing to do so, and the legally aided person will have no difficulty in finding a lawyer to take his case. He is thus at least as well placed, from the financial point of view, to seek the judicial protection of his rights as is the individual of substantial means.

To this extent it can be claimed that the English system of legal aid does ensure that the right of access to the court is available in fact as well as in theory to the poor, and most if not all of the deficiencies of the scheme are due rather to the need for economy in the use of public money than to the nature of the scheme itself. A common criticism, for example, is that the income and capital qualifications for legal aid are set too low so that many people who cannot realistically afford to meet the costs of litigation are nevertheless excluded from the scheme. And another is that legal aid extends to only two out of the large number of 'tribunals' which, though outside the regular hierarchy of the courts, are nevertheless competent to decide a wide variety of issues of great importance to the citizen. But scarcely any one argues that the appropriate extensions to legal aid should not be made as soon as economic circumstances permit: the problem is one of economic priorities, not of principle.

There is, however, one deficiency in the system just described which, while its cure may have financial implications, does also involve a matter of principle. It has been said, not inaccurately, that the legal aid scheme treats the poor man as if he were a rich man without money. In other words, it seeks to overcome the financial difficulties which are faced by the poorer sections of the community when seeking to exercise the right of access to the court, but it does little else. It is true that, today, the scheme extends to legal advice as well as to legal aid for litigation, but it has to be recognised that the poorest members of the community are likely also to be the least well informed. Frequently they will fail to realise that a problem they face has a legal dimension or that lawyers and the courts can be of assistance to them; and even if they do realise this, they are still likely to be reluctant to visit a lawyer's office and to involve themselves in the complex and sometimes intimidating processes of the law.

The problem thus raised cuts across the division between the provision of legal aid and the provision of social services in general, but in addition to non-specialist advisory organisations such as the Citizens' Advice Bureaux which are capable of recognising a legal problem, of advising an enquirer to consult a solicitor and of helping him to do so, there has recently been a development of local 'Law Centres' of one kind or another. Some of these are permanently established with one or more employed lawyers on their staffs while others are mere voluntary organisations open for a few hours a week and staffed by lawyers who give a little of their spare time without expecting payment. The former category is, obviously, capable of giving more extensive assistance than the latter, but for both the principal objective is the same, namely to provide a source of legal assistance and advice which is freely available without formality of any kind to all those in the neighbourhood who need such help. It is of particular importance that Law Centres should be situated in the more deprived areas, both because the residents of such areas are the most likely to be unable to avail themselves, through ignorance or timidity, of the regular system of legal aid operating through lawyers in private practice and also because, for obvious reasons, those areas are the least likely to contain adequate numbers of lawyers in private practice.

Although there are now almost 30 Law Centres with at least one full time lawyer and a substantial number of voluntary organisations distributed in different parts of the country, there is as yet no centralised structure and their sources of finance are varied and precarious. This is, perhaps, to be expected, for although voluntary organisations have existed for many years, the first Law Centre with a full time staff was only set up less than 10 years ago and all of those now in existence own their origins to independent local initiative. The recent Report of the Royal

Commission on Legal Services[32] does, however, make recommendations for the future which will, if they are implemented, both increase the number of Law Centres and place their organisation and their finances on a more secure footing.

The extent to which the right of access to the courts can be made a reality to the under-privileged section of the community depends ultimately on the willingness of society as a whole, both through legislation and independently of legislation, to make the necessary resources available. A major step forward was certainly taken in England after the War by the institution of the statutory legal aid scheme, and now it is generally agreed that ways must also be found of making legal assistance and advice more easily available to those who are unable, even with legal aid, to make use of the services of lawyers in private practice. Some progress along these lines has already been made and more may be expected, but there is still no way of escaping the fact that much depends on the availability of public funds, and public funds are presently in short supply. Important though 'access in fact' is now generally acknowledged to be, it cannot be a matter of absolute right. All that can be done is to seek continuous improvement in the facilities available, and to endeavour to ensure, at least when some 'fundamental' right is involved, that no one shall be prevented by poverty or ignorance from securing the protection of that right through action in the courts.

C. Civil actions in the public interest

If the phrase 'civil action' is given its traditional meaning, namely an action concerned exclusively with the private interests of the parties, then the title given to this section is paradoxical. As will appear, the paradox affects the law as it now stands, but there is no escape from the fact that the 'civil action' in the sense of an action which is civil in form, which is brought before the civil, not the criminal, court and which seeks a civil remedy, is today frequently employed in the service of the public interest as a whole or in the service of the interests of some unincorporated and loosely defined group of individuals. It is now common, for example, to find that legislation confers a right of civil action in certain circumstances on Government Departments or on statutory bodies charged with the implementation of certain legislation of a specialised kind. Thus, the Commission for Racial Equality[33] and the Equal Opportunities Commission[34] both have the right to initiate civil proceedings in their own names to restrain by injunction some kinds of unlawful discriminatory conduct and the Board of Trade, which is part of the Department of Trade and Industry, may petition the court for an

32. Loc cit. *supra*. n. 31.
33. Race Relations Act 1976.
34. Sex Discrimination Act 1975.

order that a company be wound up – a civil remedy normally available to persons such as the creditors of a company – if it appears that it is 'expedient in the public interest' that the company shall be wound up. [35]

Statutory rights of action such as these are restricted in their scope by the statutes that create them, but the right of civil action possessed by the Attorney-General, derived originally from his representation of the Crown in its capacity of *parens patriae*, has developed to the extent that, today, he may institute civil proceedings virtually whenever he considers it necessary to do so to secure compliance with the law: he may even seek a civil injunction to restrain repeated violations of the criminal law when it appears that the penal sanctions available are insufficient to deter the offender.[36]

Though civil in form, actions by the Attorney-General or by a statutory body are, of course, brought by official representatives of the public interest, but modern developments almost everywhere have created a need for the use of the civil process for the protection of the 'rights' of groups of individuals, groups which may be well- or ill-defined, and the satisfaction of this need exceeds the capacity of such 'official' rights of action as may exist. As Professor Cappelletti has said, 'human actions and relationships assume a collective rather than a merely individual character; they refer to groups, categories, and classes of people, rather than to one or a few individuals alone ... more and more frequently the complexity of modern societies generates situations in which a single human action can be beneficial or prejudicial to large numbers of people, thus making entirely inadequate the traditional scheme of litigation as merely a two-party affair.'[37] Almost everywhere in the developed world the individual or the association has begun to demand access to the court for the protection of the interests or 'rights' of groups of people or even of society as a whole, not for the protection of purely individual legal rights.

Obviously no legal system can simply allow any disaffected individual or association to bring proceedings on the alleged ground that the defendant's conduct is illegal and threatens the public interest, and the problem usually known as that of '*locus standi*' comes to the forefront. Until comparatively recently, however, English law was spared the need to seek a criterion whereby the admissibility of 'public interest' actions could be decided because of an extension to the Attorney-General's right of action which is known as the 'relator action...' [38]

35. Companies Act 1967, ss. 35, 81.
36. Of the numerous examples, see *Attorney-General* v. *Harris* (1961) 1 Q.B. 74; *Attorney-General* v. *Chaudry* (1971) 1 W.L.R. 1614.
37. 'Vindicating the Public Interest through the Courts: a Comparativist's Contribution' (1976) Buffalo Law Review 643, 646. See too Chayes 'The Role of the Judge in Public Law Litigation' (1976) 89 Harv. L.R. 281.
38. See Edwards, *The Law Officers of the Crown*, 286 et seq.

The idea of the relator action is simple. An individual or a corporation seeking to bring an action 'in the public interest' may petition the Attorney-General, and if the Attorney-General grants his consent then the action is brought in his name but, for all practical purposes, with the 'relator' as *dominus litis*. The Attorney-General does, of course, exercise a discretion in the matter, and he may be relied on to refuse his consent to actions which are worthless or frivolous, but the grant of consent to the use of his name by the 'relator' automatically resolves all problems of *locus standi*. The relator action thus provides an opportunity for the exercise of private initiative in bringing to the attention of the courts allegedly unlawful behaviour, which, while not actually injurious to private rights, is said to be injurious to the public, or to a section of the public, as a whole.

Although the Attorney-General is a political appointee and a member of the Government, it is a well-established constitutional convention that in considering whether to grant or withhold his consent to a relator action he must act objectively and without reference to political considerations.[39] No doubt, over the years, successive Attorneys-General must have refused their consent to relator actions on numerous occasions, but the system received its first challenge only in 1973, when an individual sought to bring proceedings to prevent the showing on television of a film which, he maintained, was unfit for public exhibition.[40] The action was brought against the Independent Broadcasting Authority on the ground that it had failed to perform its statutory duty in relation to the film before consenting to its exhibition, and the reason that the plaintiff acted in his own name was that it was not possible to obtain the Attorney-General's consent to a relator action in time. At a preliminary hearing the Court of Appeal agreed to hear the case and, in fact, placed a temporary ban on the display of the film. At a later hearing, by which time the Attorney General's consent had been obtained, the Court gave further consideration to the plaintiff's *locus standi* and, by a majority, agreed that in exceptional circumstances such as, for example, where there was great urgency, an action by an individual in his own name might be admitted.

In the circumstances this case was not decisive, but the question was raised in an acute form in *Gouriet* v. *Union of Post Office Workers*,[41] for in that case the Attorney-General had actually refused his consent to a relator action, and it was following that refusal that the plaintiff

39. Since 1972, local authorities have had statutory power to bring civil proceedings in their own names when they consider it expedient in the interests of the inhabitants of their area to do so: Local Government Act 1972, s. 222.
40. *Attorney-General, ex rel. McWhirter* v. *Independent Broadcasting Authority* (1973) Q.B. 629.
41. (1978) A.C. 435.

brought the action in his own name. The circumstances were politically sensitive, for the case arose out of the public announcement by the General Secretary of the defendant Trade Union that his Union would support an international week of action against the South African Government's policy of apartheid by instructing its members, employees of the Post Office, to stop all communications with South Africa for that period. Had the members of the Union complied with such an instruction they would have been guilty of criminal offences and, probably, the Union itself would have been guilty also if it had given the instruction, so Mr. Gouriet asked the Attorney-General either to take action himself to prevent this or, at least, to consent to a relator action. The Attorney-General refused both requests and Mr. Gouriet thereupon began his action in which he sought a variety of injunctions and declarations which would have had the effect of preventing the Union from going ahead with its 'action'. He expressly disclaimed any personal interest in the matter other than the interest possessed by every citizen that the postal services should continue uninterrupted and that the law should be obeyed.

At first instance the action was not admitted, and when Mr. Gouriet appealed two distinct but related questions were discussed in the Court of Appeal,[42] namely, first, whether the Attorney-General's exercise of discretion to refuse consent to a relator action could be challenged in the courts and, secondly, whether an individual might have standing to bring an action 'in the public interest' without the consent of the Attorney-General. The majority, over a vigorous dissent from Lord Denning M.R., held that the Attorney-General's exercise of his discretion could only be challenged in Parliament, but all three members of the Court agreed that in certain circumstances, including those presented in the case itself, the court could admit an action brought by an individual in his own name even though no private interest was at stake. This decision of the Court of Appeal was, in the event, sufficient to prevent the intended disruption of the postal services, but the case was later taken on appeal to the House of Lords, and the House unanimously reversed the Court of Appeal's decision.

The judgments delivered in the House of Lords are long and elaborate and they do not all agree on all aspects of the problem, but the main point on which the House decided is clear: only the Attorney-General may bring proceedings in the public interest; no individual may do so without the Attorney-General's consent, and the Attorney-General's exercise of discretion is not open to challenge in the courts. As Lord Wilberforce insisted, it is 'a fundamental principle of English law that private rights can be asserted by individuals, but that public rights

42 (1977) Q.B. 729.

can only be asserted by the Attorney-General as representing the public.'[43]

There can be little doubt that the House of Lords intended by this decision to preserve what had previously been presumed to be the rule of English law that the Attorney-General, subject only to parliamentary control, shall have the exclusive right to decide whether or not a civil action might be brought to protect the interests of a section of the public or of the public as a whole. In truth, however, that can never actually have been the rule, nor can such a rule be fully maintained in practice, for no question of the Attorney-General's consent can arise where the plaintiff can show 'interest', that is, normally, where he can show that he has suffered or will suffer damage personally as a result of the defendant's actions; and there is no way in which the motive of a plaintiff with 'interest' can be investigated. It will not infrequently be the case that an action ostensibly brought to protect the private interest of the plaintiff will in fact benefit a group of persons to which the plaintiff belongs, and there is nothing to stop him from bringing proceedings even though his motive in doing so is to benefit the group and not himself alone. This may occur for example, in 'neighbourhood' cases where one householder obtains an injunction to restrain a nuisance,[44] for the issue of the injunction is of as much value to his neighbours as it is to himself; or it may happen when the action is in reality a 'test action'. In *Congreve* v. *Home Office*,[45] for example, the plaintiff brought an action challenging the legality of a purported revocation of his television licence. Very large numbers of people had received treatment identical with that received by the plaintiff, and it was recognised by the Court of Appeal that the plaintiff was no more than the 'leader' of this group of television licence holders. The Court held that the revocation of the plaintiff's licence was unlawful, and it is beyond doubt that that decision settled the matter so far as all the other licence holders were concerned. It was, in form, a private action raising no problem of *locus standi* because the plaintiff risked the loss of £6 of his own money if the revocation of his licence were found to be valid. But no one can reasonably deny that the action was in reality an action brought in the interest of the entire group.

The possibility that a 'public interest' action may be admitted under the guise of a private action by a plaintiff with 'interest' is almost made explicit by Lord Wilberforce in a passage in his speech in *Gouriet's* case itself, for Lord Wilberforce was obliged to admit that 'a right is none the less a right, or a wrong any the less a wrong, because millions of people

43. (1978) A.C. at p. 477.
44. For a case where the grant of an injunction almost certainly was of benefit to people other than the plaintiff, see *Halsey* v. *Esso Petroleum Ltd.* (1961) 1 W.L.R. 683.
45. (1976) Q.B. 629.

have a similar right or may suffer a similar wrong.'[46] The Result of *Gouriet's* case is, therefore, not actually to ensure that the Attorney-General rather than the court shall always control the admissibility of actions brought in the public interest. If the Attorney-General's consent has been obtained and a relator action is started, no question of the action's inadmissibility can be raised, but if the Attorney-General refuses consent and an individual brings an action in his own name the court may still admit the action provided only that it can find some element of private 'right' on the part of the plaintiff. This has, in fact, always been the case even if hitherto unrealised, and many actions brought by individuals in the interest of groups of people have undoubtedly been admitted and decided without any suggestion that the plaintiff's *locus standi* might be in doubt. The trouble is that *Gouriet's* case, which brought the problem to light, effectively compels the courts to decide on the admissibility of future 'public interest' actions by reference to criteria which have no bearing on the questions which such actions actually raise.

In *Gouriet's* case the House of Lords rejected the opportunity provided by that case of beginning a development of legal principle for the solution of the problem of the admissibility of 'public interest' actions, but it did not and it could not lay down that only the Attorney-General can decide whether a 'public interest' action can be brought. It seems certain that the number of actions brought by individuals in what they conceive to be the public interest will increase; it is inevitable that the question of their admissibility is, ultimately, decided by the courts themselves. For the moment, if the Attorney-General's consent has not been obtained, the question, and thus the right of access to the court by the 'public interest' plaintiff will continue to be decided by reference to the subsidiary and, in real terms, irrelevant, question whether the plaintiff can show some element of personal damage or other 'interest', but it is predictable that the results of adhering to this inadequate solution will become more and more evidently unsatisfactory.[47] Though a unanimous and apparently unequivocal decision of the House of Lords, *Gouriet's* case cannot long remain the last word on this difficult and important subject.

46. (1978) A.C. at p. 483. Lord Wilberforce could not deny this because of the decision in *Dyson* v. *Attorney-General* (1912) 1 Ch. 158, the correctness of which was unquestioned.
47. For relevant cases decided after *Gouriet's* case, see *Ex p. Island Records Ltd.* (1978) Ch. 122; *Meade* v. *Haringey London Borough Council* (1979) 1 W.L.R. 637.

2. THE RIGHT OF PERSONAL LIBERTY

The right of personal liberty or the 'liberty of the subject' as it is often called, is no more enshrined in English legislation than any other 'fundamental' right, but its basic importance is such that two distinct and specific remedies have developed for its protection, namely the 'writ of habeas corpus' and that particular form of the civil action in tort known as the action for 'false imprisonment.' Both are, in substance, remedies for the unlawful deprivation of liberty, and it is through them that the courts have defined and controlled the powers of arrest and detention which are necessarily conferred, both by legislation and at common law, on the executive arm of government and on others. The nature and scope of these remedies will, therefore, be briefly examined in this section, but in addition mention must be made of 'release on bail', the system whereby people lawfully held in custody on criminal charges may be provisionally released pending their trials: whether it is technically correct or not to speak of a 'right' to bail, the system of release on bail makes a vital contribution in practice to the liberty of the subject.

A. The Writ of Habeas Corpus [48]

The original function of the writ of 'habeas corpus ad subjiciendum', to give it its full title, was to bring before the court an unwilling defendant or witness; its development into a procedure for protecting a person against unlawful deprivation of liberty [49] began with the constitutional struggles between King and Parliament during the seventeenth century, and by the Petition of Right of 1628 it was made available to secure the release of a person detained by order of the King. The Habeas Corpus Act 1679 provided safeguards against lengthy imprisonment without trial and contained a number of procedural improvements applicable to the case of persons detained on criminal charges; in 1816 the most important provisions of this Act were extended to other cases. It is worth noting at this point Dicey's famous observation on this legislation: 'The Habeas Corpus Acts declare no principle and define no rights'; they are 'essentially procedure Acts, and simply aim at improving the legal mechanism by means of which the acknowledged right to personal freedom may be enforced.' [50]

The modern procedure begins with an application to the court for the issue of the writ. The application is made *'ex parte'*, which means

48. For the history of the writ, see Holdsworth, *History of English Law*, IX, 108-125.
49. This development was associated, probably erroneously, with Magna Carta. See Cam, 'Magna Carta – Event or Document?', Selden Society Lecture, 1965.
50. *Law of the Constitution*, ed. 10, 199, 221.

that at this stage notice of the application to the person detaining the prisoner – the 'gaoler' – is not required. The application should be made by the prisoner himself, which will cause no problem where he is held in 'official' detention, but if for any reason the prisoner is unable to apply himself than anyone may apply on his behalf.[51] The hearing of the application takes precedence over all the other business of the court, and it is possible for an order for the release of the prisoner to be made by the court there and then. This, however, will only be done in a case where the detention is obviously and unquestionably illegal. Normally an adjournment will be ordered so that notice of the application can be given to the 'gaoler', and at the adjourned hearing the question whether or not the writ should be issued will be decided after evidence and argument on both sides. Although, technically, the issue of the writ allows the gaoler the opportunity to justify the prisoner's detention, the modern practice is to treat the hearing of the application as the full hearing of the case so that an order for the issue of the writ amounts to an order for the prisoner's release. Disobedience, which is unthinkable today where the detention is 'official', is summarily and severely punishable as contempt of court.

At the hearing the court does not consider only whether the grounds for the detention that are put forward by the 'gaoler' are sufficient in law; it also considers whether they are true as a matter of fact[52] and, though the point is not entirely clear, it appears that the burden of proof rests with the gaoler.[53] This must not be understood to mean, however, that if the justification given is that the prisoner has been sentenced to a period of imprisonment by a criminal court the court hearing the application for habeas corpus will investigate the correctness of the conviction. Habeas corpus is a remedy against unlawful detention; it is not an alternative or a supplement to the right of appeal in criminal cases.[54]

B. Action for false imprisonment

The writ of habeas corpus is a specialised remedy to secure the release of a person unlawfully detained; it is, therefore, not available to a person who has been set at liberty, no matter how he has regained his liberty and no matter how unlawful was his prior detention. The action for false imprisonment, on the other hand, is an action for damages for the civil wrong which is committed when one person unlawfully deprives another of his liberty and is thus a means whereby a person

51. Rules of the Supreme Court, 0.54.
52. *R.* v. *Board of Control, ex p. Rutty* (1956) 1 Q.B. 109.
53. See *R.* v. *Secretary of State for the Home Department, ex. p. Ram* (1979) 1 W.L.R. 148.
54. *Ex p. Hinds* (1965) 1 W.L.R. 325.

previously detained may obtain redress for the wrong done to him in the past. The title given to the action is old-fashioned and misleading; 'false' means no more than without legal justification and 'imprisonment' is not limited to detention in a place which could reasonably be described as a 'prison.' There is an 'imprisonment' whenever the victim is totally deprived of his freedom to go where he pleases and the action thus obviously covers an unlawful arrest.

In conformity with the importance which the law attaches to personal liberty, it is not necessary for the plaintiff in an action for false imprisonment to prove that his detention was unlawful: once he has proved that he was in fact deprived of his liberty by the defendant it is for the defendant to justify this if he can.[55] Nor is it necessary for the plaintiff to prove that he suffered any significant damage as a result of his detention or even that he was aware of it at the time.[56] The mere fact of unlawful deprivation of liberty is sufficient, and substantial damages may be awarded. In one of the cases of the eighteenth century in which the plaintiff had been detained for a matter of six hours only, during which he had been well treated, very substantial damages were awarded for what the court described as ' a most daring public attack made upon the liberty of the subject.'[57]

Obviously no action for false imprisonment and no application for the writ of habeas corpus can succeed if the detention was lawful, as it certainly will be if it followed the conviction and sentence of a criminal court or a lawful arrest. The case of convictions presents no difficulty, but the law concerning arrest otherwise than in pursuance of a warrant of arrest issued by a magistrate is complex. Much of it is, today, contained in legislation,[58] but there is no single statute dealing with the subject as a whole, and even taking all the relevant legislation together it still does not approximate to a code. Much has been and much still is left to clarification by the courts, and the occasions for this clarification are most commonly in actions for false imprisonment or in applications for habeas corpus.[59]

In approaching their task the courts are, of course, aware of the need to maintain public order and safety, and sometimes they will even go beyond the literal meaning of the statutory words to meet this need. In one case,[60] for example the driver of a car was arrested by police

55. *Dallison* v. *Caffery* (1965) 1 Q.B. 348.
56. *Meering* v. *Grahame-White Aviation Co. Ltd.* (1920) 122 L.T. 44.
57. *Huckle* v. *Money* (1763) 2 Wils. 205.
58. In particular the Criminal Law Act 1967.
59. Actions for false imprisonment contributed, with other forms of civil actions for tort, to judicial declarations in the eighteenth century of the illegality of 'general warrants', i.e. warrants for arrest, search, and so on which purport to authorise the arrest of persons by describing them generally instead of specifying them by name and giving particulars of the offence with which they are charged.
60. *Wiltshire* v. *Barrett* (1966) 1 Q.B. 312.

officers who considered him to be unfit to drive through drink. He was taken to a police station where, after examination, he was declared fit to drive by a doctor whereupon he was released without being charged with any offence. In his subsequent action for false imprisonment the police officers relied on a section of an Act of Parliament which provided, first, that a person who drives or attempts to drive a car while unfit through drink commits an offence and, secondly, that 'a police constable may arrest ... a person committing an offence under this section.' The plaintiff contended that since he had committed no offence his arrest must have been unlawful, but the court held that it was sufficient justification that the police officers had believed, honestly and upon reasonable grounds, that the offence was being committed: the need to protect the public against the dangers of drunken driving demanded that interpretation of the legislation. On the other hand, at least where an immediate arrest is not necessary for the protection of the public, a stricter rule will normally be applied. Thus, for example, it is recognised as a general principle that unless the circumstances make it impossible, a man must be told of the reason for his arrest at the time the arrest is made. In *Christie* v. *Leachinsky* [61] police officers had arrested the plaintiff and had professed to do so for a reason which was, as a matter of law, insufficient to justify an arrest without warrant. They were held liable for false imprisonment notwithstanding that valid reasons for the plaintiff's arrest without warrant actually existed.

One of the most prolific sources of applications for habeas corpus in recent years has been the detention with a view to expulsion from the country of persons alleged to be illegal immigrants or of aliens whose presence is alleged to be prejudicial to the public interest. In both classes of case the applicable legislation confers wide discretionary powers on the Executive and the powers of the court are thus somewhat restricted, but they will at least ensure that the legal requirements are meticulously observed and, in the case of illegal immigrants, will order the detained person's release unless it is made to appear that 'a reasonable Secretary of State, acting upon the information available *to the court* and to the Secretary of State, could have acted as he did in ordering the detention that he did.' [62] In cases concerning the deportation of aliens, however, the needs of national security – a matter for the executive not the judicial branch – may compel the court reluctantly to conclude that it cannot intervene. As Lord Denning M.R. said in a recent decision, [63] 'There is a conflict here between the interests of

61. (1947) A.C. 573. See also *John Lewis & Co. Ltd.* v. *Tims* (1952) A.C. 676 where it is laid down that an arrested person must be brought before a magistrate as soon as possible.

62. *R.* v. *Secretary of State for the Home Department* (1979) 1 W.L.R. 148, 154, *per* May J. Emphasis added.

63. *R.* v. *Secretary of State for Home Affairs, ex p. Hosenball* (1977) 1 W.L.R. 766, 783.

national security on the one hand and the freedom of the individual on the other. The balance between these two is not for a court of law. It is for the Home Secretary.'

It cannot be claimed for English law, therefore, that judicial protection of the 'right' to personal liberty is always available, but to admit this is no more than to admit that English law does not recognise an absolute right to personal liberty, and that is an admission that honesty would extract not only from an English lawyer but also from a lawyer in a country whose written Constitution purported to endow its citizens with such a right. No modern state can dispense altogether with discretionary powers of arrest and detention, nor can it insist that only a duly constituted court of law can lawfully deprive a man of his liberty. Whether the approach is by way of a constitutional declaration of right or by way of the provision of legal remedies, the end result need not be different, for it makes little difference whether the court is called upon to decide whether an exception to the constitutional right to liberty justifies detention in a given case or whether the court begins by enquiring whether the plaintiff has suffered a legal wrong. What is important for the protection of liberty is the availability of recourse to the courts so that the legality of the detention in the particular case can be tested.

C. Release on 'bail'

On the face of things a person who has been lawfully arrested on a criminal charge or who has been remanded in custody by a court pending his trial is not unlawfully deprived of his liberty. He cannot, therefore, complain of a false imprisonment and, subject to what is said below, he cannot obtain his release by way of the writ of habeas corpus. It is however, an important maxim of the criminal law that a man is to be presumed innocent until his guilt of a particular offence has been proved before a court, and the necessity of keeping some persons in custody until their trial thus conflicts with the principle that a man whose innocence is to be presumed should not be deprived of his liberty. The resolution of the conflict, so far as English law is concerned, lies in the system of 'bail.' A person is said to be released 'on bail' when he is granted liberty pending his trial (or, perhaps, the hearing of an appeal).

In the early days of the common law a man accused of serious crime was usually released pending his trial as soon as sureties to secure his appearance in court could be found. According to the legal historians Pollock and Maitland,[64] however, this was not due to any love of

64. *History of English Law*, II, 584.

abstract justice but because imprisonment was costly and troublesome and medieval prisons were easy to break out of. In course of time, however, the system of release on bail came to be linked with the principle that an accused man should retain his liberty until conviction unless there were good reasons to the contrary, and over the years there has been a good deal of legislation concerning both the nature of the offences in respect of which bail should or should not be granted and the character of the 'bailors' or sureties who should be required to answer for the accused's appearance at his trial.[65]

In modern procedure the prosecution of minor offences begins with a mere 'summons' to the accused to appear before the court; he is never taken into custody and so no question of bail arises. Where a person is arrested, on the other hand, he must be brought before a magistrates' court as soon as possible and the magistrates will then deal with the matter of bail. If the accused person was arrested without a warrant, however, his release on bail may be considered even before he is brought before a court: the officer in charge of the police station to which the accused is taken may, and, if the accused cannot be taken before a court within 24 hours, must himself enquire into the case and, exceptionally serious cases apart, must release the accused on bail, requiring him to appear before a magistrate's court at a stated time and place.[66]

Once the accused comes before the court, whether he has previously been granted bail or not, the whole matter of bail is open to the court, and the way in which the court's discretion should be exercised has been the subject of considerable controversy and of a number of statutory changes in modern times. The point, of course, has been to try to strike the right balance between the competing claims involved – on the one hand the importance of releasing on bail persons who have, as yet, been convicted of no offence and, on the other, the importance of ensuring that accused persons do not abscond, do not commit further offences and do not attempt to interfere with the administration of justice by, for example, attempting to suborn witnesses.

It is not possible to enter into this controversy here, save to say that the present law as contained in the Bail Act 1976 creates a strong presumption in favour of the grant of bail. Indeed, the Act provides in terms that a person who is accused of an offence *shall be granted bail* when he is brought before a court or when he applies for bail unless the court decides that it should refuse bail on one of a very limited number of grounds, the most important of which is that the court is satisfied that there are *substantial* reasons for believing that if the accused per-

65. See Holdsworth, *History of English Law*, IV, 526-528.
66. Magistrates' Courts Act 1952, s. 38.

son were released on bail he would fail to surrender to custody before trial, would commit a further offence or would attempt to interfere with potential witnesses.[67]

The Act of 1976 is intended to keep to a minimum the number of persons detained in custody pending trial, and as a further means of achieving this it has made a major departure from the former practice. In the past it was the almost invariable practice not only to demand sureties but also to require the accused person himself to enter into a recognisance, that is, in effect, to provide a bond or deposit which would be forfeit if he failed to surrender; inability to provide the required recognisance involved the accused person remaining in custody. Now, however, this system has been abolished;[68] in its place a new offence, that of 'absconding by a person released on bail' has been created, and for this offence a person is liable to a fine or imprisonment or both. He may of also, of course, be rearrested.[69]

In the past it was possible for a person refused bail by a lower court to make use of the procedure of habeas corpus in order to seek release on bail from a superior court[70] and this may still be so today.[71] It has, however, for long been accepted that the superior courts have power to release a person on bail *virtute officii*. Today it is provided by statute that if an inferior court refuses to release an accused person on bail then the High Court or the Crown Court may grant bail itself.[72] The procedure is simple:[73] the applicant issues a summons directed to the prosecutor calling upon him to show cause why bail should not be granted, and the judge's decision is final. Moreover, to safeguard the interests of ignorant or indigent accused persons it is laid down that if magistrates refuse bail they must inform the accused of his right to apply to the higher court; and if a person held in custody wishes to do so but is unable to instruct a solicitor to act for him through lack of means he may give notice of this to the judge. The judge may then, if he thinks fit, assign the official solicitor to act for the prisoner and the application for bail may be dealt with in a summary manner without even the necessity for a summons.

The Bail Act 1976 came into force in April 1978, and, at least during the years leading up to it, there had been some dissatisfaction at the working in practice of the bail system; it appears that an unfortunately

67. Bail Act 1976, s.5(1) and Schedule 1. Emphasis added. Note the significant substitution of the word 'substantial' for the more usual 'reasonable'.
68. *Ibid.*, s. 3(2).
69. *Ibid.*, ss. 6, 7.
70. The Habeas Corpus Act 1679 made provision for the release on bail of persons charged with treason or felony if they were not brought to trial within a reasonable time.
71. See *In re Kray* (1965) Ch. 736.
72. Criminal Justice Act 1967, s. 22; Courts Act 1971, s. 13.
73. See Rules of the Supreme Court, 0.79, r.9; Crown Court Rules 1971 rr. 17, 18, 22.

large number of accused persons who were actually acquitted at their trials or who, though convicted, did not receive custodial sentences had been kept in custody pending trial.[74] The reforms of the new Act should improve the situation, especially those aimed at informing accused persons of their rights under the system and, of course, the introduction of the principle that bail should be granted unless there are strong and specific reasons to the contrary. Nevertheless, it is inevitable that in many cases the decision whether or not bail should be granted must depend upon a number of imponderable factors so that, ultimately, much depends on the attitudes adopted by the many magistrates in the country upon whom the prime responsibility for operation of the bail system rests. It may be that in recent years those magistrates have been over-reluctant to release in a case of doubt, but there is now at least an awareness of the problem and a fresh appreciation of the relevance of bail to the overall protection of the liberty of the subject. As the Lord Chancellor said in an address to magistrates in 1971, 'The Bench has to balance the rights of the public against the rights of the individual. It may (or may not) be that the rights of the public are more important. But the wrong to the individual, namely the deprivation of his right to liberty, is more certain, and, where he is innocent, can be more serious.'[75]

3. FREEDOM FROM DISCRIMINATION

Notwithstanding the absence of any constitutional text, it is now many years since English law rid itself of all laws which overtly discriminated against persons on account of their race, creed or colour, all the remaining disabilities, and in particular those relating to religious affiliation, having been abolished during the nineteenth century. Nor, from the procedural point of view, does the law any longer give, as it formerly did, any special privilege to the Crown or other public authority as a party to litigation before the courts. In 1947 the immunity of the Crown from liability to be sued for tort was swept away,[76] and in 1954 the especially favourable periods of limitation which formerly applied when an action was brought against a public authority were abolished.[77] That the law itself does not discriminate, however, does not

74. See e.g. Bottomley, 'The Granting of Bail: Principles and Practice' (1968) 31 M.L.R. 40; Bottomley, *Prison before Trial*; Zander, 'A Study of Bail/Custody Decisions in London Magistrates' Courts' (1971) Crim. L.R. 191.
75. *Law Guardian*, No. 74 (1971) 9; (1971) 121 New L.J. 825.
76. Crown Proceedings Act 1947. It remains impossibile to bring proceedings against the Sovereign in person. Trade Unions are afforded special immunities: Trade Unions and Labour Relations Act 1974, s.14.
77. Law Reform (Limitation of Actions, etc.) Act 1954, repealing the Public Authorities Protection Act 1893.

mean that it protects those who are discriminated against by others, and it is with that matter that this section is concerned. It is necessary to consider separately the non-statutory or common law on the subject and the modern legislation relating directly to discrimination on the ground of race or sex.

A. The Common Law

The extent to which the common law can protect persons against discrimination is severely limited by the basic freedom of every individual to decide for himself with whom he wishes to associate or contract. Since I am free to sell my house to whomsoever I choose and also to decline to sell it altogether, the common law can in the nature of things give no redress to a person to whom I refuse to sell it even though the reason for my refusal is that he is coloured; since I am free to employ whomsoever I choose, I commit no unlawful act if I refuse to employ a man because he is a Jew. In other words, the common law can only intervene to prevent discrimination if there is some independent legal basis upon which it can proceed.

It does appear, however, that within the limits of the possible, the common law has set its face against discrimination on racial grounds. In one of the best known cases, for example, a coloured man sought accommodation at a hotel, and was refused. The hotel, being in law a 'common inn', was under a common law duty to receive and provide accommodation for travellers to the extent that it had vacant accommodation, and the court held that it was liable for breach of this duty.[78] In another case trade union officials instructed their members, who were musicians, to refuse to play in the orchestra at a public dance hall for so long as the proprietors of the dance hall refused to admit coloured persons. This action by the union officials was prima facie unlawful as a conspiracy to interfere with the trade of the proprietors of the hall, but it was held that the purpose of bringing the colour bar to an end provided a legal justification.[79] In various cases where legacies have been made subject to conditions designed to exclude certain classes of person from benefit on the basis of racial or religious discrimination, the courts have refused to give legal validity to those conditions.[80] Finally, it is probable that restrictive covenants limiting the use or future disposition of land which, in principle, bind not only the original parties but also subsequent owners of the land in question,

78. *Constantine* v. *Imperial Hotels* (1944) K.B. 693.
79. *Scala Ballroom (Wolverhampton) Ltd.* v. *Ratcliffe* (1958) 1 W.L.R. 1057.
80. E.g. *Clayton* v. *Ramsden* (1943) A.C. 320; *In re Lysaght* (1966) Ch. 206.

would be held to be ineffective if they purported to restrict future sales of the land to members of certain racial groups.[81]

Potentially the most far-reaching common law development in this area, however, came in a case involving discrimination not on account of race but on account of sex. In *Nagle* v. *Feilden*[82], the plaintiff, a woman, had applied for and been refused a licence as a trainer of race horses by the defendant stewards of the Jockey Club, and she brought her action for a declaration that this refusal was unlawful being, as she alleged, based solely upon the ground that she was a woman. The Jockey Club, though not a body having any powers conferred upon it by the law does, for all practical purposes, exercise monopoly control over horse racing and no horse may be raced at any major race meeting unless it has been trained by a licensed trainer. On a preliminary application to strike out the plaintiff's action on the basis that even assuming her allegations to be true no legal right of hers had been infringed, the Court of Appeal held that her action must be allowed to proceed. In the words of Lord Denning M.R., 'The common law of England has for centuries recognised that a man has a right to work at his trade or profession without being unjustly excluded from it. He is not to be shut out from it at the whim of those having the governance of it. If they make a rule which enables them to reject his application arbitrarily or capriciously, not reasonably, that rule is bad. It is against public policy. The courts will not give effect to it'. Too much must not, of course, be made of this case; but if its spirit is followed the common law may find that it has after all a weapon at its disposal for use against at least the more blatant exercises of discrimination by those bodies, whether statutory or not, which exercise effective de facto control over entry to a given trade or profession.[83]

B. Legislation

Obviously much of the general criminal law, especially that relating to crimes of violence, may be invoked after incidents in which people have been attacked on account of their race, and severe sentences have been passed in some such cases. In addition, for what it may be worth, the victims of such attacks are entitled to bring civil actions for damages for tort. Until comparatively recently, however, no legislation specifically aimed at discrimination existed. Even now, though the volume of anti-discriminatory legislation is substantial, the only use made of

81. *Noble and Wolf* v. *Allen* (1951) D.L.R. 321, a decision of the Supreme Court of Canada.
82. (1966) 2 Q.B. 633.
83. See further *David* v. *Abdul Cader* (1963) W.L.R. 834; *Faramus* v. *Film Artistes' Association* (1964) A.C. 925.

the criminal law has been the creation of a specific offence of incitment to racial hatred which was first introduced in 1965.[84]

The beginning of anti-discriminatory legislation in England, a modest one, came with the Race Relations Act 1965; this declared 'unlawful' discrimination on the ground of colour, race or ethnic or national origins, but only if the discrimination occured in relation to places of 'public resort' such as hotels, places of entertainment and public transport. A Race Relations Board and local conciliation committees were created, and the general technique for enforcement of the legislation was to seek voluntary compliance without use of the legal process. Judicial protection of the 'right' to freedom from discrimination was, therefore, not available, but the Attorney-General was given power in certain rather limited circumstances to bring civil proceedings for an injunction to restrain continuing or repeated acts of unlawful discrimination.[85]

The Race Relations Act 1968, which replaced that of 1965, considerably enlarged the scope of unlawful discrimination, extending it to the supply of goods and services generally, to employment and to housing. In addition it introduced an individualised legal remedy, though a limited one: the Attorney-General's right to sue for an injunction was transferred to the Race Relations Board which was also given the right to sue for damages on behalf of a person who had suffered loss in consequence of an act of unlawful discrimination. The injured person himself could not bring proceedings nor was he a party to proceedings brought by the Board, but at least a first step towards judicial protection of the 'right' was taken.[86]

In 1975 Parliament enacted the Sex Discrimination Act allowing far more elaborate and individual methods of enforcement, and this Act was followed a year later by the Race Relations Act 1976 which replaces the Act of 1968 and which uses much the same enforcement techniques as the Sex Discrimination Act on which it is modelled. These two Acts contain the principal anti-discriminatory legislation which is now in force.

The Sex Discrimination Act created the 'Equal Opportunities Commission' and the Race Relations Act 1976 transformed the old Race Relations Board into the larger and more powerful 'Commission for Racial Equality.' Each Commission is charged with the implementation of the Act of Parliament appertaining to it. For obvious reasons, the

84. Race Relations Act 1965. s. 6. For a case in which a violently anti-semitic speech was held to constitute an offence before the Act of 1965 was passed, see *Jordan* v. *Burgoyne* (1963) 2 Q.B. 744.

85. Race Relations Act 1965, s. 3.

86. Race Relations Act 1968, ss. 19, 21, 22. The Board had, of course, to account to the injured person for any damages recovered.

law relating to discrimination on the ground of sex, on the one hand, and of race, on the other, is not in all respects the same. Nevertheless, at the level of broad generalities, the similarities are more important than the differences, and the two Acts may be considered briefly together.

The core of each Act lies in the definition of 'discrimination', the essence of which is that one person discriminates against another if he treats that other less favourably than he treats or would treat other persons on the ground of race or sex as the case may be; both Acts extend the definition to cover the application to a person of a requirement or condition which, though equally applicable to others, is such that the proportion of persons of the same race or sex who can comply with it is considerably smaller than the proportion of persons not of that race or sex.[87] It is not, of course, the case that all forms of discrimination are made unlawful by one or other of the Acts, but their scope, especially in the fields of employment, education and the supply of goods, services, facilities and premises is now extensive. In a recent case,[88] for example, it was held that unlawful discrimination on racial grounds had occurred when a (white) barmaid was dismissed from her employment in a public house because she would not accept her employer's instructions to refuse to serve coloured customers; and in another[89] it was actually held that a rule operating in a factory, according to which the women were allowed to leave their work five minutes before the men, amounted to unlawful discrimination against the men.

It is neither possible nor necessary here to consider closely the substantive provisions of either Act; suffice it to say that the extent of the notion of unlawful discrimination is now such that it is possible to say that English law recognises a 'right' to non-discrimination on grounds of race or sex. What is of importance for present purposes is that, although the legislation continues to place considerable reliance on extra-judicial enforcement including both conciliation and investigation by the appropriate Commission followed, if necessary by the issue of a 'non-discrimination notice', that is a notice requiring the person to whom it is addressed to give up acts found to be discriminatory,[90] there is also

87. Sex Discrimination Act 1975, ss. 1, 2, 3, 4; Race Relations Act 1976, ss. 1, 2 'Racial grounds' as defined in the Act means 'colour, race, nationality or ethnic or national origins': *ibid.*, s. 3(1). Note that the application of a 'requirement or condition' will not amount to unlawful discrimination if it is shown to be justifiable irrespective of the sex or race, etc. of the person to whom it is applied. This allows, for example, the application of a condition of high educational qualifications, if these are necessary in the circumstances, even though far fewer members of one racial group than of another will be able to comply with the condition.

88. *Zarczynska* v. *Levy* (1979) 1 W.L.R. 125.

89. *Peake* v. *Automobile Products Ltd.* (1977) Q.B. 780.

90. For 'non-discrimination notices' and their effects, see Sex Discrimination Act ss. 67-71; Race Relations Act, ss. 58-62.

widespread availability of judicial remedies. The Commissions themselves may, in certain circumstances, bring proceedings for an injunction or declaration and, most significantly, an individual personally affected by an act of unlawful discrimination may bring proceedings in his own name.[91] If he was affected in his employment then his action should be in the industrial tribunal, otherwise in the ordinary courts. The Commission itself may assist the individual litigant if the case involves a point of principle or if in the circumstances it is unreasonable to expect him to proceed unaided.[92] As a general rule the court may award damages. including compensation for injured feelings, and a variety of declarations and orders. In addition, if a person has been dismissed from his employment on the ground of race or sex, his dismissal will have been 'unfair' within the meaning of the Trade Union and Labour Relations Act 1974 and so, provided that he has been in the employment for at least 26 weeks, the Industrial Tribunal will be able to order his reinstatement.[93]

91. Sex Discrimination Act ss. 63-66; Race Relations Act ss. 54-57.

92. Sex Discrimination Act, ss. 74, 75; Race Relations Act, ss. 65, 66.

93. Trade Union and Labour Relations Act 1974, Schedule 1, paras. 4-15; Employment Protection Act 1971, s. 71.

Part III

Public and Private Law: The Role of the Courts

The distinction between public and private law features prominently in both the Digest and the Institutes of Justinian.[94] It also plays an important practical role in the working of many modern legal systems. For the Romans the distinction probably had no technical significance but was rather one of the general classifications they had learnt from Greece,[95] and it may be, therefore, that the contemporary importance of the distinction is attributable more to the insistence of the French revolutionary legislators on a strict separation of powers[96] than to adoption of ideas apparently contained in the Roman text but, however this may be, the view is generally accepted that where the State is involved, then, the matter arising cannot be dealt with as if both parties were private individuals. One need do no more than cite the opinion of the French Tribunal des Conflits in the famous *'Blanco'* case of 1873[97] when it said, of the liability of the State for damage, that the liability 'has its own special rules which vary according to the needs of the service and the necessity to reconcile the rights of the State with private rights.'

There is, however, nothing theoretically inevitable about the distinction, and in England it has, generally speaking, 'exclusively academic and educational significance.'[98] No doubt there is much in English law that is conveniently classified as 'public law' including, obviously 'constitutional' and 'administrative' law, and the distinction is of value for a number of scholarly and pedagogic purposes. The critical question here, however, is whether it actually controls the decision of any concrete case: certainly it does not, as it does elsewhere, control the division of competence between one jurisdiction and another.

It was one of the cardinal features of Dicey's concept of the Rule of Law in England[99] which he contrasted sharply but not altogether accurately or fairly with what he found in France – that the same rules of law apply to all and that no distinction is made between private individ-

94. D. 1.1.1.2; J.1.1.4.
95. See Jolowicz, *Roman Foundations of Modern Law*, 51.
96. See Law of 16-24 August 1790, art. 13.
97. Feb. 8, 1873. D. 1873, III, 20.
98. Kahn-Freund and others, *A source book of French Law*, 182.
99. Dicey, *Introduction to the Study of the Law of the Constitution*, (ed. 10) Cap. 4.

ual and government official. In the context of 'fundamental rights' the most important application of this is found in the law of tort, and the point to which Dicey attached great importance was that a public servant who acts unlawfully and causes damage may be sued by the victim of the damage in the ordinary courts and in accordance with the ordinary law even though the unlawful act took place in the course of the public service. Dicey seems to have attached surprisingly little importance to a major exception to this which existed throughout his lifetime, namely the rule that might be described as, itself, a rule of 'public law', that the Crown could not be sued for tort at all and could only be sued for breach of contract if the Attorney-General granted his 'fiat' for a 'Petition of Right.' This exception has, however, been almost entirely removed by the Crown Proceedings Act 1947, the key provision of which so far as the law of tort is concerned is that as a general rule 'the Crown shall be subject to all the liabilities in tort to which, if it were a private person of full age and capacity, it would be subject.'[100]

The far-reaching effect of this may be illustrated by reference to the case of *Dorset Yacht Ltd.* v. *Home Office,*[101] in which the Home Office – a department of the Crown – was sued in respect of damage to property which had been caused by young deliquent boys who had escaped from custody: it was alleged that the boys had been enabled to escape by the negligence of the officers responsible for them and that the Home Office was liable for that negligence. The action was thus framed as an ordinary action in tort for negligence.

To the case thus put the Home Office replied, in effect, that the boys were detained under statutory authority, that it had a wide discretion in determining the conditions of their detention and that it was essential that various methods of retraining them should be used including that of leaving the boys relatively free from close and continuous supervision. Liability for negligence under the ordinary principles of the law of tort requires that the defendant shall have broken a 'duty of care' owed to the plaintiff, and if it were the law that the Home Office owed a duty of care to persons such as the plaintiff in the case, this would mean that it could not freely exercise its discretion in the performance of its public duty of retraining and rehabilitating young delinquents.

The argument that the Home Office should thus be held immune from liability for negligence was rejected by the House of Lords. As was pointed out by the House, it was not 'negligence' on the part of persons in charge of delinquent boys merely to give them a certain or even a substantial amount of freedom. The duty of care required only that the officers should exercise their discretion reasonably and that they should

100. Crown Proceedings Act 1947, s. 2.
101. (1970) A.C. 1004.

take such care for the protection of the property of others as is consistent with the performance of their functions. In other words, the actual principles of law applicable to the case were no different from those applicable to any other case in which negligence is alleged; those principles require that in measuring the standard of care required and in determining whether or not the duty of care has been broken all the circumstances of the case must be taken into account, and in the case of persons in charge of delinquent boys those circumstances include the nature of the statutory duties imposed upon them, but that is all.

It is not intended to suggest that even now the Crown and other public bodies are treated by the law in all respects in the same way as private persons. It is still the rule, for example, that no injunction may be issued against the Crown,[102] and there are situations in which the act of a public authority is concerned for which no private analogue exists.[103] Nevertheless it seems to be generally true that the tendency of the law is towards unity and that the spirit of the Crown Proceedings Act is being adhered to, consciously or unconsciously, in cases to which it has no direct application: the principles of law are the same, whatever the character of the parties to the litigation. The case of *Attorney-General* v. *Jonathan Cape*[104] provides a recent example. The Attorney-General sought an injunction to prevent the publication of the diaries of the late Richard Crossman, a former Cabinet Minister. The diaries included accounts of Cabinet meetings and indicated the opposing views expressed by individual Cabinet Ministers, some of whom, including the Prime Minister himself, were still in public life when the action was brought. The Attorney-General claimed, therefore, that publication of the diaries, and of the information acquired by Mr. Crossman under the confidence of the Cabinet Room, would be contrary to the public interest because of the threat that it would present to the constitutional principle of collective Cabinet responsibility. No such action had ever been brought before the courts before, but certain principles had been developed in relation to breaches of confidence between private individuals. The Lord Chief Justice had no hestitation in applying those principles, adapted to the particular circumstances before him, for the purpose of his decision.[105]

The tendency to unity of the law is not only to be seen in the use of

102. Crown Proceedings Act 1947, s. 21. But an order declaratory of the rights of the parties may be made in lieu.

103. A proviso to s. 2 of the Crown Proceedings Act specifies that the Crown shall not be liable if the act in question would not have given rise to a cause of action against the individual responsible for it.

104. (1976) Q.B. 752.

105. In addition to cases involving commercial secrets the Lord Chief Justice relied in particular on *Duchess of Argyll* v. *Duke of Argyll* (1967) Ch. 302 which concerned domestic confidences passing between husband and wife.

'private' law principles for the solution of 'public law' cases; principles developed in the 'public' sphere have also been adopted for the solution of 'private' or, at least, 'non-public' cases. Thus, to give but one example, organisations as different as trade unions and universities exercise extensive power over individuals and may make decisions vitally affecting individual interests: expulsion from a trade union may deprive a man of his livelihood; universities exercise disciplinary powers up to and including the expulsion of students. To deal with these and similar cases the courts have not merely assumed a jurisdiction to review the decisions of these organisations but in exercising that jurisdiction they apply principles which are, for all practical purposes, the same as those used for the review of the decisions of statutory and other 'public' bodies.[106]

In these circumstances it is surprising that in the case of *Gouriet* v. *Union of Post Office Workers*[107] the House of Lords should have chosen to base its decision to exclude the plaintiff's action on the distinction it asserted between 'public' and 'private' rights and on its insistence that only the Attorney-General, as sole representative of the public interest, may seek to enforce the former in the courts. It is also disappointing, at least if the decision is taken at its face value, for, as Cappelletti has said, the 'massification' of society has led to the result that it is no longer plausible to insist that the law deals only with relationships between individual and individual, on the one hand, and between individual and the State, on the other. 'Today's reality is much more complex than that abstract dichotomy: between the individual and the State there are numerous groups, communities and collectivities which forcefully claim the enjoyment of certain rights which are classifiable neither as 'public' nor as 'private' in the traditional sense.'[108] And Cappelletti cites the words attributed to Pietro Verri in the eighteenth century which are almost uncannily apposite for the conditions of today: 'the last to see clearly the interests of society are those who are paid to do so.'[109] The judicial protection of all but purely individual 'private' rights cannot safely be left in the hands of the official representatives of the public interest alone; subject to appropriate conditions which must urgently be devised, others also must be entitled to invoke the jurisdiction of the courts, for the courts cannot themselves ever take the initiative.[110]

106. See e.g. *Breen* v. *Amalgamated Engineering Union* (1971) 2 Q.B. 175; *Glynn* v. *Keele University* (1971) 1 W.L.R. 487.
107. (1978) A.C. 435, *ante*, Part II, 1., C.
108. 'Vindicating the Public Interest through the Courts' (1976) 25 Buffalo Law Review 643.
109. The quotation is from Verri's *Pensées detachées*. See Cappelletti in Cappelletti and Jolowicz, *Public Interest Parties and the Active Role of the Judge*, 93.
110. See *Attorney-General* v. *Independent Broadcasting Authority* (1973) Q.B. 629, 656-657, *per* Lawton L.J.

What, then, is the role of the courts? Traditionally, and in simple terms, the role of the court in any given case is to apply the law to the facts and produce the appropriate conclusion together with any order or decree that the law may require. This calls for a meticulous examination of the facts and the authoritative solution of controverted questions of fact, and it is to that aspect of the court's role that the greatest importance commonly attaches in practice. This is as true of cases involving 'fundamental' rights as it is of others. From a more general point of view, however, it is the notion of the 'application of the law' that is the more critical and the more complex. The moment that we abandon the fiction that 'the law' is permanently complete and exists independently of its application in individual cases we are forced to acknowledge that the judge is not a mere automaton whose conclusion, once the facts are determined, follows as a matter of simple logic. Whether we see 'the law' as being contained wholly in the words of the legislator or whether we see it, as common lawyers are still prone to do, as what Justice Holmes once called 'a brooding omni-presence in the sky', the process of 'applying the law to the facts' will frequently demand of the judge an element of what, for want of a better word, may be called 'judgment.' If we are honest, we must admit that judges are employed to exercise their judgment in the cases presented to them.

When we speak of the judicial protection of rights, therefore, we cannot be content to see the role of the courts as being merely that of protecting rights which have been defined, more or less precisely, by the legislature and it is, of course, the fact that the common law has for long recognised the authority of judicial decisions as sources of law even if it has only quite recently abandoned the fiction that judges do not make law. Recognition that judges make law does not mean, however, that the law of Parliament and the law of the judges operate in the same way. Legislation emanates from a body which is recognised as constitutionally entitled to make law, and legislation comes, inevitably, in the form of a text. The text may be clear or unclear and may call for much or little by way of 'interpretation' before it can be applied to concrete circumstances by the judges, but the one thing that can never be said of a legislative text is that it does not correctly state the law. This is not true of any statement or formulation of a rule or principle of case law.

The common law judge does, as is well known, support his decision by an elaborate explanatory judgment in the course of which he examines previous decisions on the point and, frequently, quotes the actual formulations of the law which his predecessors have adopted; he also, frequently, offers a formulation of his own adapted to the particular facts before him. None of these formulations is, however, the equivalent of a legislative text and, despite the emphasis sometimes given in academic circles to the authority of the single precedent and the problem of discovering the *ratio decidendi* of *a* case, it is extremely rare in practice that the law on a point is to be found otherwise than through the examination of a number of decisions. No formulation of rule or principle by a judge can be other than provisional; its accuracy as a statement of the law can only be tested by reference to the cases that are decided after it was given. It is through the steady and continuous accretion of decisions rather than through the formulations adopted by individual judges that the law develops. [111]

In the field of 'fundamental' rights as in others, therefore, we look to the judges for two things. First, we look to them to provide the appropriate remedy when a wrong has been done and, secondly, we look to them for the development of the law at all levels of generality and detail, development that comes through their decisions in one case after another. And because, in reality, much may depend on the way in which the judge's preconceptions and inarticulate premises influence his reaction to the case presented to him, we cannot blind ourselves to the fact that the character of the judge – his professional character conditioned more by the legal environment in which he has been educated and in which he has lived his life than by his individual personality – will influence what he does. The power of the individual judge to give shape and direction to the law is not always great, for the reasons just given, but, at least in a common law system, the power of the judges as a whole to do so and to give substance to the aspirations of a society through their decisions is very great indeed.

This power is not, however, without its limits, though the limits are difficult if not impossible to define save in the vaguest of terms. [112] It is certain, for example, though the explanation is not, that it was beyond the powers of the judges to overcome the ancient rule that the Crown was not answerable for the torts of its servants: that necessary change had to wait for legislative intervention which finally came through the Crown Proceedings Act of 1947. Of present importance is the undoubted limit on the power of the judges that is implicit in the doctrine of the supremacy of Parliament, namely that Parliament may both undo what the judges have done [113] and place specific limits on their powers for the future. This leads to the question of 'constitutionalisation' or the introduction into English law of a 'Bill of Rights' to which attention is shortly given in the concluding Part of this paper.

111. For a fuller discussion of this analysis of the case law process, see Jolowicz, 'Les décisions de la Chambre des Lords' (1979) *Revue internationale de droit comparé*, 521.

112. This is an important subject which is in need of study. The obvious statement that the courts must not usurp the function of the legislature gives little guidance.

113. The most notorious example is the passage of the War Damage Act 1965 to reverse retroactively the effect of the decision of the House of Lords in *Burmah Oil Co. Ltd.* v. *Lord Advocate* (1965) A.C. 75. See Jolowicz, 'Fundamental Guarantees in Civil Litigation: England' in Cappelletti and Tallon (ed.) *Fundamental Guarantees of the Parties in Civil Litigation*. 123, 131-134.

Part IV

Constitutionalisation of Fundamental Rights[114]

The concept of the supremacy of Parliament has been the subject of much discussion by constitutional lawyers and by legal theorists, but for present purposes it is unnecessary to give to it a meaning wider or more complex than that the courts must, subject only to their power of interpretation, give effect to whatever Parliament enacts. The supremacy of Parliament in this sense was not always clearly accepted as part of English law, and in *Dr. Bonham's* case[115] in 1610 Sir Edward Coke indicated that the courts could declare an Act of Parliament to be void if they found it to be contrary to reason. This is, in effect, to treat the common law, that is, the law independent of legislation, as equivalent to a fundamental or higher law which limits the powers of Parliament itself. Attractive though this may be to some, no such idea has been tenable in England in modern times.[116] That Acts of Parliament are absolutely binding on the courts was graphically illustrated as recently as 1973 when the House of Lords refused even to consider the question whether the passage of an Act by Parliament had been secured by the deception of Parliament.[117] Lord Reid regarded the idea that a court could disregard a provision in an Act of Parliament as one that 'must seem strange and startling to anyone with any knowledge of the history and law of our constitution';[118] Lord Morris stated firmly that 'it is the function of the courts to administer the laws which Parliament has enacted.'[119]

It is against this background that the suggestion that certain rights should be 'constitutionalised' or included in a 'Bill of Rights' must be considered, and the first question to which the suggestion gives rise is whether a law of constitutional status, that is, a law which would be secure against subsequent repeal by Parliament, is capable of enactment

114. There is already a considerable volume of literature on the possibility of introducing a Bill of Rights into English law. See Wallington and McBride, *Civil Liberties and a Bill of Rights*, the bibliography at Appendix 5 and, in addition, Dahrendorf, 'A confusion of Powers: Politics and the Rule of Law' (1977) 40 M.L.R. 1; Milne, 'Should we have a Bill of Rights?' *ibid.*, 389; Mann, 'Britain's Bill of Rights' (1978) 94 L.Q.R. 512 (the European Convention); Duncanson, 'Balloonists, Bills of Rights and Dinosaurs' (1978) Public Law 391. It is not possible to consider this literature here, and what follows represents only the writer's reflexions on the matter from the particular point of view of the subject of this paper.
115. (1610) 8 Co. Rep. 113b.
116. See e.g. *Lee* v. *Bude and Torrington Junction Railway Co.* (1871) L.R. 6 C.P. 576.
117. *Pickin* v. *British Railways Board* (1974) A.C. 765.
118. *Ibid.*, at p. 782.
119. *Ibid.*, at p. 789.

and if so by what means. Such is the concept of parliamentary supremacy as generally understood that even if one Parliament were to provide that an Act incorporating certain fundamental rights could not be repealed or could only be repealed by a special majority, that would not be binding on its successors: the courts would be obliged to give effect to the later, repealing, Act.

This obstacle is not necessarily insuperable and, for the purposes of what follows, it will be assumed that it could be overcome or, alternatively, that the problem is more theoretical than real: once a Bill of Rights had been enacted, even by way of an 'ordinary' Act of Parliament, the political obstacles to its repeal would be so great as to render it for all practical purposes a permanent feature of the law. The important question is whether a Bill of Rights would make a valuable contribution in the particular context of English law in the late 20th Century.

Until comparatively recently the suggestion that England or, rather, the United Kingdom, should be endowed with a written constitution of any kind was virtually unthinkable. Written constitutions might be required elsewhere either because the country concerned had found it necessary to set down principles on its coming into existence as an independent nation after a period of colonial rule or because recent experience had indicated the need to place formal restrictions on the powers of the legislature: and, of course, a federal state needs a constitution at least to allocate competences between the federation itself and its constituent parts. The United Kingdom was not, and is not, a federal state, and its long history of parliamentary government had, it was assumed and asserted, produced a sufficiency of political and other controls to render unnecessary the creation of a system of judicial control of legislation; and judicial control of legislation is, ultimately, the principal legal consequence of a written constitution.[120]

Over the last twenty years or thereabouts, a body of opinion has developed which opposes this attitude as a result, at least in part, of the fear that the political controls of Parliament have become inadequate. In particular, some consider that the effect of the Party system as it has become has been to make Britain what the present Lord Chancellor once called 'an elective dictatorship'; as another distinguished judge has observed, 'when times are abnormally alive with fear and prejudice, the common law is at a disadvantage: it cannot resist the will, however frightened and prejudiced it may be, of Parliament.'[121]

120. It is not a necessary consequence as is shown, for example, by the experience of France. Note, however, that though judicial review of parliamentary legislation remains impossible in France, the Conseil Constitutionnel, which may consider certain legislation before promulgation, has begun to develop some of the characteristics of a constitutional court. For a valuable account in English of this development, see Nicholas, 'Fundamental Rights and Judicial Review in France' (1978) Public Law 82, 155.
121. Scarman, *English Law – the New Dimension*, 15.

The argument is thus essentially one for strengthening the powers of the courts, and for this reason it comes into conflict with the contrary argument that the action of any court which annuls or otherwise declines to apply a parliamentary enactment is inevitably anti-majoritarian and undemocratic. It also raises the spectre of the judge compelled to enter into the political arena and to resolve issues which are essentially of a political, non-justiciable, kind. The possible use of the 'Brandeis brief' as developed in the United States, which would provide the judges with information going far beyond that normally considered necessary for the solution of legal issues, would provide a partial answer to this, but it would not remove the evil, if evil it be, of entrusting to judges questions which call for the judgment of elected representatives, not of supposedly apolitical judges, and it would not avoid the danger that some commentators see of putting in peril the independence of the judiciary itself.

It is not proposed to consider further this particular controversy. It is one upon which indefinite argument is possible; its resolution depends for each individual on his own assessment of the various opposing values which are involved, and that assessment will in turn depend on the individual's political views, will vary almost from one moment to the next, and will, in any case, be affected by the actual content of any proposed Bill of Rights. There are, however, certain other aspects of the general question to which a lawyer can properly draw attention without giving undue weight to his own political convictions.

Apart from introducing the possibility of the annulment of legislation, experience in other countries, in particular the United States, suggests that recognition in a constitutional text of certain broadly stated rights enables the courts to develop procedural and other safeguards at a level of some detail which they might otherwise be unable to do: it is unnecessary to do more than mention the numerous decisions of the Supreme Court of the United States which proceed from the 'due process' clauses of the Fifth and Fourteenth Amendments.[122] On the other hand this advantage of constitutionalisation and, indeed, the advantage of judicial control of legislation itself – if that be an advantage – depends ultimately on the way in which the judges envisage their own function and on the way in which they perform it. It is idle to pretend and dangerous to suppose that the mere statement of certain broad principles is capable of its own motion of securing the protection of any right or the maintenance of any value; it is also idle if not actually dangerous to suppose that any such statement is capable of compelling judges by the force of deductive logic alone to reach particular solutions

122. See e.g. *Gideon* v. *Wainwright* 372 U.S. 335 (1963); *Boddie* v. *Connecticut* 401 U.S. 371 (1971). Cf. *U.S.* v. *Kras* 409 U.S. 434 (1973); *Ortein* v. *Schwab* 410 U.S. 656 (1973).

in particular cases. The most that can be said is that it may provide the judges with a formal basis for decisions which, it is assumed, will favour the protection of the rights which are enumerated.

From the practical point of view the choice for the United Kingdom between retention of its present system and the introduction of a Bill of Rights seems essentially to be the choice between continuing to leave the final control to Parliament itself and transferring to the courts a power to give preference to the enumerated rights and values over the will of Parliament. For a lawyer it is tempting to suppose that the protection of, at least, the traditional 'fundamental' rights is better left to judges than to politicians, and the experience of other countries seems to show that at certain periods of history the introduction of judicial review of legislation under a 'rigid' constitution becomes a necessity: it is an open question whether the United Kingdom has entered upon such a period. But, while there are certainly educational values for a society in the clear constitutional statement of certain rights and values as being basic to the society, there is also serious danger in encouraging the belief that those rights and values are capable of protection and maintenance by the law and the courts alone. The preservation of 'fundamental' rights depends upon the operation and co-operation of every element that contributes to the character of a society, and while the law is an important element it is by no means the only one. It may well be the case that the educational function of the introduction of a Bill of Rights in the United Kingdom would prove in the result to be its most important.

The phrase 'Human Rights and Fundamental Freedoms' as used, for example, in the European Convention, is a highly emotive one, and the protection of those rights and freedoms is, obviously, something for which all right-minded human beings must strive. It has, however, been the theme of this paper that the distinctive contribution that the law itself can make is through its decisions in individual cases, hypothetical as well as actual, and that the casuistical approach is the characteristic one of the common law. As stated early in this paper, the English idea of law is essentially court-orientated and so, generally speaking, it accommodates more easily the concept of 'wrong' than that of 'right'. This does not mean that English judges could not adapt their intellectual approach so as to make satisfactory use of a catalogue of 'rights' such as would appear in a Bill of Rights, but it almost certainly does mean that their reaction would be to use the Bill of Rights as a means for deciding whether or not some action, especially the actual passage of an Act of Parliament, was wrongful, that is, unlawful. Only if it has become clear that the existing extra-legal controls of legislation that have been developed over the centuries have now ceased to give satisfactory results is the lawyer entitled to call for so major a transfer of power from Parliament to the courts.

It is not unlikely that this approach to the possible introduction of a Bill of Rights and, indeed, the approach to the problem of 'fundamental rights' in general which has been adopted in this paper will fail to appeal to many lawyers and even to many English lawyers, especially those who have specialised in 'public' law. This paper is, however, the product of one whom those concerned to classify would surely classify as a 'private' lawyer and who, perhaps in consequence, is persuaded that too much must not be expected of the law. The law is but one strand in the complex web of factors which shapes a society, and the contribution that the law can make to the preservation of the rights and freedoms that we value is not by the reiteration of sweeping generalisations which the harsh realities of life cannot fail immediately to qualify the moment that they come to be applied. It is for the politicians, for the teachers and for the men of religion to speak in generalities; it is for the lawyer to attend to detail and, in particular, to ensure that wrongs are not left unredressed. It is mainly a matter of national psychology or, at least, of the characteristics of national legal systems, whether that object is best achieved by the enunciation of rights or the development of remedies for wrongs, but undoubtedly it is the latter approach which has provided the chief inspiration of English law throughout its history. As Sir Ivor Jennings once wrote, 'There is no more a "right of free speech" than there is a "right to tie up my shoe-lace"; or, if there is a right of free speech, there is also a right to tie up my shoe-lace. The question to be discussed in each case is the nature of the legal restrictions.'[123] Or, as Megarry V.-C. put it, 'England, it may be said, is not a country where everything is forbidden except what is expressly permitted: it is a country where everthing is permitted except what is expressly forbidden.'[124] It is for the law to say what is forbidden, and freedom demands that only those things which must be forbidden in the interests of freedom itself shall be forbidden by the law.

The protection of freedom rarely allows the law to speak in absolutes; the law must find the individual solutions which differing circumstances require and, though the enunciation of principles in legislative form may help, it has hitherto been the English experience that it is more profitable for the law to identify, and redress the harm done by, acts which should be and are forbidden, than to speak formally in general terms. When all is said and done, that is all that the law as law can do, and it is to the availabilty and accessibility of judicial remedies that the professional lawyer concerned with 'Fundamental Rights and Human Freedoms' should principally direct his attention.

123. *The Law and the Constitution*, 243.
124. *Malone* v. *Metropolitan Police Commissioner* (1979) Ch. 344, 357.

THE INFILTRATION OF EQUITY INTO ENGLISH COMMERCIAL LAW

by

G. Jones

The Infiltration of Equity into English Commercial Law

The Role of the Trust

From time to time attempts have been made to introduce equitable doctrine into the corpus of English commercial law. For example judges have occasionally flirted with the concept of a 'trust of a promise', in an attempt to enable C to sue on a contract which A had made with B for his benefit. But the flirtation was shortlived. There was no easy answer to the artificial question, when did B hold his right to sue A on trust for C? [1] Moreover, to imply such a trust would generally be quite inconsistent with the commerical expectations of A and B since it would mean they could never vary or revoke the terms of the contract even though they might subsequently wish to do so.[2]

The doctrine of constructive notice also made its bow. But the initial reception was very chilly indeed. In *Manchester Trust* v. *Furness,*[3] a charter party contained a proviso that the captain and crew of a ship should be the servants of the charterers, and that the captain should only sign bills of lading as their agent. The charterers agreed to indemnify the owners against any liability arising from the captain signing bills of lading. However, the captain signed the bills of lading in the ordinary form, whereby the holders agreed to pay 'freight for the same and other conditions as per charter'. The goods were misdelivered; and an action was brought by holders of the bills of lading against the owners for the loss. The owners argued that the holders must look to the charterers to satisfy their claim. They had constructive notice of the special stipulations in the charterparty, in particular that the captain was the agent of the charterers, not the owners, when he signed the bills of lading. The Court of Appeal unanimously and unequivocally rejected that argument. As Lindley L.J. said:[4]

> 'There is no doctrine that goes to anything like that extent; and as regards the extension of the equitable doctrines of constructive notice to commercial transactions, the Courts have always set their faces resolutely against it. The equitable doctrines of constructive notice are common enough in dealing with land and estates, with which the Court is familiar. But there have been repeated protests

1. See Glanville Williams, (1944-1945) 7 Modern Law Review 123.
2. Cf. the observations of Lord Denning M.R. in *Beswick* v. *Beswick* [1966] Ch. 638, 555.
3. [1895] 2 Q.B. 539.
4. At p. 545.

against the introduction into commercial transactions of anything like an extension of those doctrines, and the protest is founded on perfect good sense. In dealing with estates and land title is everything, and it can be investigated; in commercial transactions possession is everything, and there is no time to investigate title; and if we were to extend the doctrine of constructive notice to commercial transactions we should be doing infinite mischief and paralyzing the trade of the country.'

Recently these wise words have been ignored. A bookmaker was made a constructive trustee of £135, the proceeds of a number of cheques made payable to him and drawn on a fiduciary account, because he failed to inquire whether the fraudulent executor was acting properly in drawing these cheques on the account.[5] More significantly, banks, acting for a company and an individual in the course of a takeover transaction, have been declared to be constructive trustees of money passing through these accounts because they should have realized that that individual was using the company's own money to acquire the company's shares,[6] a transaction which is illegal under the English Companies Act 1948.[7] These decisions are not easy to reconcile with earlier authority[8]; and there are now dicta of the Court of Appeal which reconfirm that the doctrine of constructive notice should have no application in these circumstances and that a bank or a stranger will only become a constructive trustee if it or he consciously facilitates a breach of trust.[9] To require a bank *to investigate* the propriety of a fiduciary's conduct would be to impose an unreasonable burden on it, remembering how stringent is its obligation to honour the cheques of its customers.[10]

Possession should be everything; 'and there is no time to investigate title'.[11] It is for this reason too that a good faith purchaser of a negotiable instrument need make no inquiry whether his vendor was in a position to give good title.[12] As Lord Brougham once said: 'The negligence of the party taking a negotiable instrument does not fix him with the defective title of the party passing it to him.'[13]

5. *Nelson* v. *Larholt* [1948] 1 K.B. 339.
6. *Selangor United Rubber Estates Ltd.* v. *Cradock (No. 3)* [1968] 1 W.L.R. 1555; *Karak Rubber Co. Ltd.* v. *Burden (No. 2)* [1972] 1 W.L.R. 602.
7. Companies Act 1948, s. 54.
8. *Gray* v. *Johnston* (1868) L.R. 3 H.L.1. *Shields* v. *Bank of Ireland* [1901] 1 I.R. 222, 232-233, *per* Porter M.R.
9. *Carl-Zeiss Stiftung* v. *Herbert Smith & Co.* [1969] 2 Ch. 276, 296, *per* Sachs L.J., 301, *per* Edmund Davies L.J., *Belmont Finance Corp. Ltd.* v. *Williams Furniture Ltd.* [1978] 3 W.L.R. 712, 728, *per* Buckley L.J., 734, *per* Goff L.J.
10. *Gray* v. *Johnston* (1868) 3 H.L. 1.
11. *Manchester Trust* v. *Furness* [1895] 2 Q.B. 539, 545; *ante* p. 51.
12. *London Joint Stock Bank* v. *Simmons* [1892] A.C. 201.
13. *Bank of England* v. *Fagan* (1849) 7 Moo. P.C. 61, 72, cited in *London Joint Stock Bank* v. *Simmons [1892] A.C. 201, 219, 221,* per Lord Herschell.

An equally firmly rooted principle of commercial law is that creditors should be protected from undisclosed charges over the property of their debtors. It should be a natural corollary of that principle that one creditor should enjoy priority over another only if his debt is secured and is seen to be secured. For that reason the English Companies Act 1948 requires that charges over the property of a company must be registered; if they are not the holder will simply rank as a general creditor.[14] In *Coptic Ltd.* v. *Bailey,*[15] a successful attempt was made to subvert this principle through the equitable doctrine of subrogation. In that case A lent some money to a company, B, to enable B to buy land from C. The loan was secured by a legal mortgage on the land in A's favour; but the mortgage was not registered. Nevertheless Whitford J. allowed A to be subrogated to the unpaid vendor's lien of C. This was a most unfortunate decision since it frustrated the policy of the Companies Act and gave A a security (the lien) in equity even though he had not registered his mortgage. For these reasons Walton J. refused to follow it in the later case of *Burston Finance Ltd.* v. *Speirway*[16] and on identical facts, very properly, refused to allow A to be subrogated to C.

The courts have not always been as sensitive to the claims of general creditors. For example, on occasion, they have found that a contract between businessmen created not only a 'debt' but also a trust of specific assets for the benefit of the plaintiff. The implications of such a conclusion are most significant. A bank cannot set off a customer's debt against a credit (a chose in action) which it knows that its customer holds on trust for another.[17] Again, under the Bankruptcy Act 1914 identifiable property held by a bankrupt as trustee for another does not pass to the bankrupt's trustee in bankruptcy.[18] The existence of a trust is then a rock for the general creditors of the bankrupt. It can be too a hidden rock: for it may be that, on the particular facts, no reasonable investigation could have revealed that assets held by a bankrupt were held by him on trust for another.[19] Moreover, assets held on trust for another do not normally fall within the so-called 'reputed ownership' clause of the Bankruptcy Act.[20] They will only do so if the beneficiary permits his trustee, who subsequently becomes bankrupt, to deal with the property in a manner inconsistent with the trust; and it will be rare that this will be found to be the case.[21]

14. s. 95 (1).
15. [1972] Ch. 446.
16. [1974] 1 W.L.R. 1648.
17. *Barclays Bank Ltd.* v. *Quistclose Investment Co.* [1970] A.C. 567.
18. s. 38 (1).
19. Cf. *post* pp. 54-55.
20. s. 38 (4).
21. The cases are discussed in Williams on *Bankruptcy* (18th ed.), pp. 329-330. Moreover the 'reputed ownership' clause has no application in the winding up of companies.

In many situations the contest is between general creditors of a debtor and a person who claims that the debtor is his trustee, in circumstances where it is said that the trust arises because the creditor and debtor intended also to create a trust.[22] But a trust may also be created unilaterally, by a debtor, for the benefit of a creditor who remains blissfully unaware of its existence. Such was *Re Kayford.*[23] The Kayford Company which carried on a mail order business was in considerable financial difficulties. Its managing director became concerned for those customers who had sent money for goods which, he rightly feared, the company might not be able to supply. After taking advice, the company opened a 'Customer Trust Deposit Account', into which all further sums paid by customers for goods were deposited. 'The object of doing this was that if the company had to go into liquidation, these sums of money could and would be refunded to those who had paid for them.'[24] Subsequently the company did go into voluntary liquidation. Megarry J. held that the money in the Customer Trust Deposit Account did not form part of the general assets of the company but was 'held in trust for those who paid it.' The liquidators were 'unable to contend that any question of a fraudulent preference arose.' For this was a case 'not of preferring creditors but of preventing those who pay money from becoming creditors, by making them beneficiaries under a trust.' The 'whole purpose' of the transaction was to ensure that the monies remained in the beneficial ownership of the customers. Such a trust could be created by the customers themselves or, as in *Re Kayford*, by the company. 'If either is done, the obligations with respect of the money are transformed from contract to property, from debt to trust.'[25]

The judge did not make it clear why the liquidators could not claim that there was a fraudulent preference. But the implication of his reasoning is that the customers could not be preferred as creditors because they had ceased to be, if they ever were, creditors. There is no doubt that a debtor, such as the *Kayford* company, may create a trust of indentifiable assets for the benefit of a customer. But the debt owed by the company to the customer does not disappear with the creation of the trust. The *Kayford* debts would have only disappeared if the customers had agreed that their debts should be released in consideration of the creation of the trust. There was no such novation because the customers were in complete ignorance of the trust. Consequently the creation of the trust must have amounted to a preference of certain creditors, the 'depositors', to other creditors. Indeed, the decision is

22. Cf. *Barclays Bank Ltd.* v. *Quistclose Investment Co.* [1970] A.C. 567.
23. [1975] 1 W.L.R. 279.
24. At p. 280.
25. At pp. 281-282.

doubly objectionable for it elevates them to the position of secured creditors in circumstances where they had not bargained for any security.[26] What is also disturbing is that it is unlikely that the existence of the *Kayford* trust could ever have been discovered, on reasonable investigation, by persons who subsequently gave credit to the company. The only clue would have come from knowledge of the existence of the equivocally worded, 'Customer Trust Deposit Account.'

Re Kayford is, however, an exceptional case. It is rare for a businessman to prefer one set of customers over another simply because he thinks it 'just' to do so. The trust which was successfully used in the *Romalpa* case[27] is commercially far more significant; for it provides a mechanism for an unpaid seller, who has parted with possession of his goods, to retain title to the goods, their product and the proceeds of sale, until he has been paid *all* the sums owed to him by the buyer. The plaintiffs were a Dutch company which manufactured aluminium foil in the Netherlands. They sold quantities of foil to the defendants, an English company carrying on business in England. The contract was written in Dutch; but the court's interpretation of it was inevitably based on an English translation.[28] The conditions of the contract were said to be subject to the Dutch law; but no evidence was adduced to suggest that its principles were different from those of English law.[29] The critical clause of the general selling terms and conditions provided

26. Cf. *Coptic* v. *Bailey* [1972] Ch. 446, criticised *ante* p. 53.
27. The full title is: *Aluminium Industrie Vaasen B.V.* v. *Romalpa Aluminium Ltd.* [1976] 1 W.L.R. 676.
28. The clause reads in Dutch as follows:
De eigendom van het door A.I.V. te leveren materiaal gaat eerst op koper over zodra deze al hetgeen hij uit welken hoofde ook aan A.I.V. verschuldigd is, aan A.I.V. heeft voldaan. Tot aan het tijdstip van betaling is koper gehouden dit materiaal op te slaan op een wijze die het als eigendom van A.I.V. kenbaar doet zijn, indien A.I.V. zulks verlangt. A.I.V. en koper komen overeen dat, indien koper van het materiaal (een) nieuw(e) voorwerp(en) vormt of doet vormen, dit materiaal met (een) ander(e) voorwerp(en) vermengt of indien dit materiaal op enigerlei andere wijze bestanddeel wordt van (een) ander(e) voorwerp(en) A.I.V. de eigendom van dit (deze) nieuwe voorwerp(en) zal verkrijgen tot zekerheid van de volledige betaling van het door koper aan A.I.V. verschuldigde.

A.I.V. en koper komen daartoe reeds nu overeen, dat de eigendom van bedoeld(e), al dan niet voltooid(e) voorwerp(en) aan A.I.V. zal/zullen worden overgedragen en dat deze eigendomsoverdracht geacht zal worden plaats te hebben door en op het tijdstip van de enkele handeling of gebeuren waardoor het materiaal wordt omgevormd tot (een) nieuw(e) voorwerp(en), dan wel vermengd wordt met of bestanddeel wordt van (een) ander(e) voorwerp(en). Tot aan het tijdstip van de volledige betaling van het door koper aan A.I.V. verschuldigde zal koper de (het) desbetreffende voorwerp(en) houden voor A.I.V. in diens hoedanigheid van fiduciair eigenaar en desverlangd dit (deze) voorwerp(en), als zodanig kenbaar, opslaan. Koper zal niettemin gerechtigd zijn deze voorwerpen in het kader van zijn normale bedrijfsuitoefening aan derden te verkopen en te leveren, met dien verstande dat – indien A.I.V. zulks wenst – koper, zolang hij niet volledig aan zijn betalingsverplichtingen tegenover A.I.V. heeft voldaan, de uit deze verkopen aan koper tegenover zijn afnemers toekomende vorderingen aan A.I.V. zal overdragen.
29. I am informed by Judge Willems that this was an unfortunate assumption. *Fiduciair eigenaar* do not mean that the manufacturer is a trustee. The 'words go back to the Roman law concept of fiducia cum creditore.'

that: 'the ownership of the material to be delivered by [the plaintiffs] will only be transferred to the [defendants] when [they have] met all that is owing to [plaintiffs] ... Until the date of payment [the defendants can be required], if the plaintiffs so desire, to store this material in such a way that it is clearly the property of [the plaintiffs].' The concluding part of the clause dealt with the situation which would arise if the purchaser mixed the aluminium foil with other materials for the purpose of creating 'new objects'. The plaintiffs were given ownership of these new objects 'as surety of the full payment of what [the defendants] owe [the plaintiffs].' Until 'full payment' the defendants were required to keep the 'new objects' in their 'capacity of fiduciary owner.'[30] Nevertheless they could sell them, though they were required to assign to the plaintiffs the benefit of any claim against any sub-purchasers if they had not discharged in full their indebtedness to the plaintiffs. Subsequently the defendants got into serious financial difficulties. A receiver was appointed by the debenture holders. It was admitted that the plaintiffs were the owners of the unsold aluminium foil held by the receiver. The sole issue before the court was as to the fate of £35, 152 which represented the proceeds of the sale of unmixed aluminium foil supplied by the plaintiffs to the defendants and sold by the defendants to third parties. This sum had been segregated by the receiver to await the decision of the court.

The Court of Appeal, upholding Mocatta J., held that the defendants were in a fiduciary relationship to the plaintiffs. Accordingly the plaintiffs were entitled to trace the proceeds of sale and, having done so, they took those proceeds in priority to the secured and unsecured creditors of the defendants. The Court concluded that the effect of the agreement between the plaintiffs and the defendants was to create for the plaintiffs' benefit a trust of the unsold aluminium foil and also of any fund which represented the proceeds of sale of the foil. The Court of Appeal accepted that this interpretation did 'destroy the benefit' of a 75 days period of credit which the plaintiffs had allowed the defendants, particularly since the property in the foil, any 'new objects' or proceeds of sale was to remain in the plaintiffs until *all* the sums owing by the defendants, whenever incurred, had been paid. The Court was not persuaded by the argument that the trust, if established, successfully avoided the requirement that a hidden charge was effectively created and that a charge over the book debts of the company must be registered.[31] Nor was it conclusive that the creation of a trust would inevitably produce for companies in the position of *Romalpa* acute cash flow problems and that day-to-day business would be virtually impossible since until all debts were paid off the company could only use the

30. Ante n. 29.
31. Companies Act 1948, s. 95 (1).

proceeds of any sale for the sole purpose of 'paying the plaintiffs.' To interpret a contract in this way would be to look at the contract solely from the point of view of the defendants. The question was what did *the parties* intend to do. In the Court's view the plaintiffs' intention was that they intended to create a trust, not a charge, so that they should never be in the position of a creditor. That was their object in drafting the clause. The defendants had agreed to this. Any argument that the clause should be construed in order to give effect to the 'business efficacy' of the contract had to give way to that agreement. [32]

The commercial implications of *Romalpa* are disturbing for the very reasons which the Court of Appeal regarded as irrelevant. It would appear that, through the creation of a hidden trust, the plaintiffs succesfully created for themselves a position more favourable than that enjoyed by a secured creditor who would be required to register his charge if he were to retain its priority. Megaw L.J. thought that it was sufficient answer that the Court was simply interpreting a commercial transaction made between businessmen with equal bargaining power. [33] But that was not in issue. The real contest in *Romalpa* was not between the plaintiffs and the defendants but between the plaintiffs and the defendants' secured and unsecured creditors, who could never have discovered that assets which *appeared* to be part of the defendants' stock in trade belonged in equity to the plaintiffs.

Many commercial enterprises have sought to take advantage of the Court of Appeal's interpretation of the *Romalpa* clause, In *Borden (U.K.) Ltd.* v. *Scottish Timber Products Ltd.*, [34] the plaintiffs had supplied resin to the defendant under a contract which contained a reservation of title clause. The defendant used it to make ship board. Judge Rubin found that the defendant received the resin as a bailee for the plaintiffs; consequently a fiduciary relationship was created. So applying the tracing rules formulated in *Re Hallett's* case,[35] he held that the plaintiffs could trace their resin into the ship board. The contract gave the defendant power to use the resin in the manufacture of goods but *not* to hold any goods so manufactured to its own account; in particular the use of the resin in the process of manufacturing of ship board did not mean that the plaintiff lost his property, thereby putting an end to the right to trace. (The Court of Appeal has reversed his decision. The contract was one of sale and purchase subject to the of title clause).[35a]

In *Re Bond Worth Ltd.*, [36] however, Slade J. significantly limited the

32. [1976] 1. W.L.R. at pp. 689-670, *per* Roskill L.J.
33. This appears from the fuller report in [1976] 2 All E.R. 552, 567.
34. '*The Times*', November 15 1978.
35. (1880) 13 Ch. D. 696, on which see Hanbury and Maudsley, *Modern Equity*, p. 565 *et seq.*
35a. The judgments of the Court are now reported [1979] 3 W.L.R. 672.
36. [1979] 3 W.L.R. 629.

scope of the *Romalpa* decision. *Monsanto* had supplied *Bond Worth* with large quantities of acrylic fibre, which was then blended into yarn for carpets, to the value of some £110.000 per week. *Bond Worth* became hopelessly insolvent and the question arose whether their receivers could retain the *Monsanto* acrylic fibre and also the cash which represented sales by *Bond Worth* of carpets containing *Monsanto* fibre. The judge concluded that the construction of *Monsanto's* contract with *Bond Worth* was critical. He distinguished *Romalpa* on the ground that *Bond Worth* was *not* a bailee of the acrylic fibre. They were 'ordinary buyers' and the property in the fibre passed to *Bond Worth* 'at the latest when it was delivered.' 'The implicit authority and freedom of *Bond Worth* to employ the relevant raw materials, products and other monies as it pleased for its own purpose during the subsistence of the operation of the retention of title clause were ... quite incompatible with the existence of a relationship of *Bond Worth* as trustee and *Monsanto* as beneficiary solely and absolutely entitled to such assets.' Slade J. considered that such cases as *Foley* v. *Hill*[37] and *Henry* v. *Hammond*[38] were clear authority 'for the proposition that, where an alleged trustee has the right to mix tangible assets or monies and to deal with them as he pleases, this is incompatible with the existence of a *presently* subsisting fiduciary relationship in regard to such particular asset or money.' The contract demonstrated that the parties did not intend to create a trust, whereby *Bond Worth* was to be the trustee and *Monsanto* the sole beneficiary. Unlike *Romalpa* the contract did not reserve to the supplier the legal and beneficial interest in the fibre until the full payment of the purchase price. What the parties were intending to do was to create an equitable charge over the present and future assets of *Bond Worth* to secure repayment of the monies from time to time owing to *Monsanto* by *Bond Worth* if *Bond Worth* subsequently were to fall into financial difficulty. Consequently the charge should have been registered under the Companies Act 1948, s.95 (1); not having been registered, it could not take effect as a secured charge.

The implications of *Romalpa* are disturbing. Slade J's decision in *Re Bond Worth* is a sensible and neat circumvention of the *Romalpa* decision. However, it appears that the judge was only able to reach his decision because he was able to conclude as a matter of construction that *Monsanto* had not retained the legal and beneficial title to the fibre. A company which slavishly follows the *Romalpa* contract would still be protected by it. But it appears that Slade J. had doubts whether *Romalpa* could be reconciled with earlier precedent, not apparently

37. (1848) 2 H.L.C. 28.
38. [1931] 2 K.B. 515.

cited, which holds that a right to mix tangible assets, delivered by the plaintiff, with one's own property is inconsistent with the creation of a 'presently subsisting fiduciary relationship in regard to such particular assets' and, therefore, with the creation of a trust.

The Role of the Injunction

Only in very exceptional cases will an English court compel a defendant specifically to perform a commercial contract.[39] Damages are generally deemed to be an adequate remedy. It is not surprising, therefore, that a party to a contract will rarely obtain an injunction to restrain the other party to the contract from breaking it. He will be able to do so if the contract is specifically enforceable. But, even if it is not, he may succeed if the defendant threatens to break a *negative* term of his contract with the plaintiff: for example, that he will not sing for another impressario during the term of his contract with the plaintiff.[40] The courts have acted cautiously in granting such injunctions; in practice they have generally been granted to restrain breaches of contracts for personal services although injunctions to prevent the breach of commercial contracts are not unknown.[41]

It is a different and more difficult problem if the plaintiff seeks to enjoin not the other party to the contract but a third party, a stranger, who acquires 'by gift or purchase ... property from another, with knowledge of a previous contract' made between the original contracting parties.[42] The litigation has normally arisen in two distinct, if complementary, contexts –

a. A sells goods to B, obtaining from him an undertaking that if the goods are resold they should be resold only at a certain price. B resells the goods to C, taking from him a similar undertaking. C proposes to sell, or sells to, D at a lower price.

b. A agrees to hire B for a specific period of time a chattel, such as a ship. A sells the chattel to C who buys it with knowledge of (or subject to) the contract of hire.

English courts have consistently refused to enforce price maintenance agreements against a third party, C, where C is in no contractual relationship with A.[43] But they have occasionally indirectly enforced, through the injunction, a condition restricting the use of a chattel, for example, when C has bought a ship with actual knowledge that it is

39. See, generally, Hanbury and Maudsley, *Modern Equity*, chapter 2.
40. *Lumley* v. *Wagner* (1852) 1 De G.M. & G. 604.
41. *Sky Petroleum Ltd.* v. *V.I.P. Petroleum Ltd.* [1974] 1 All E.R. 954.
42. *De Mattos* v. *Gibson* (1858) 4 De G. & J. 276, 282, *per* Knight-Bruce L.J.
43. *Taddy & Co.* v. *Sterious & Co.* [1904] 1 Ch. 354; *McGruther* v. *Pitcher* [1904] 2 Ch. 306.

already under charter to another.[44] In one such case[45] Knight Bruce L.J. was of the opinion that 'the acquirer [C] shall not, to the material damage of the third person, in opposition to the contract [between A and B] and inconsistently with it, use and employ the property not allowable to the giver and seller.' These observations have been restrictively interpreted; indeed it has been said that they are heretical in that, if adopted, they would enable A to compel C, through an injunction, *not* to 'do something' in circumstances where A had had no proprietary interst to protect and where there was no contract between A and C.[46] However in *Swiss Bank Corporation* v. *Lloyd's Bank Ltd.*[47] Browne-Wilkinson J. treated them as 'good law' and as authority for the proposition that 'a person proposing to deal with property *in such a way as to cause a breach of a contract affecting that property* will be restrained by injunction from so doing if when he acquired that property he had actual knowledge of that contract'.[48] Knight Bruce L.J.'s principle was, in the judge's view, 'the counterpart in equity of the tort of knowing interference with contractual rights'.[49] Few would dissent from the conclusion that an injunction may be granted to restrain a stranger from inducing a contracting party to break his contract with the plaintiff or from interfering with a contract to which he is not a party.[50] But the authorities do not go beyond this, so as to embrace the situation where a stranger, C, disposes of certain property knowing that the disposition would infringe the terms of B's contract with A, in circumstances where B acted *properly* in transferring that property to C. It is not critical that B has exacted from C a promise which is the same as that given by B to A; A still cannot sue because he is not a party to the contract between B and C.[51] A would even fail even if he were B's undisclosed principal[52], for he would have given no consideration for the promise made to him (through B's agency) by C.[53] In the leading case of *Dunlop* v. *Selfridge*[54], Lord Dunedin, a Scotsman educated in the civil law, confessed that this result nipped 'any budding affection ... for the doctrine of consideration. For the effect of that doctrine ... is to make it possible for a person to snap his fingers at a bargain deliberately

44. *Lord Strathcona Steamship Co. Ltd.* v. *Dominion Coal Co.* [1926] A.C. 108. This was in fact a decision of the Judicial Committee of the Privy Council.
45. *Ante* n. 42.
46. *Port Line Ltd.* v. *Ben Line Steamers Ltd.* [*1958*] 2 Q.B. 146, 168, *per* Diplock J.
47. [1979] 2 All E.R. 853.
48. [1979] 2 All E.R. 853, 874, *per* Browne-Wilkinson J.; italics supplied.
49. *Ante* n. 48.
50. *Manchester Ship Canal Co.* v. *Manchester Racecourse Co.* [1901] 2 Ch. 37.
51. *Dunlop Pneumatic Tyre Co. Ltd.* v. *Selfridge & Co. Ltd.* [1915] A.C. 847.
52. On undisclosed principals, see B.S. Markesinis and R.J.C. Munday, *An Outline of the Law of Agency*, pp. 118-119.
53. *Ante* n. 51.
54. [1915] A.C. 847, 855.

made, a bargain not in itself unfair, and which the person seeking to enforce it has a legitimate interest to enforce.' The development of English law has therefore been stultified by its insistence that a plaintiff should succeed only if he still has property which the restrictive condition is designed to protect; *or* if the plaintiff and the defendant had contracted with each other and the plaintiff has given consideration for ('bought') the defendant's promise to him. At one time it appeared that English law would adopt a much more generous principle; namely, that if a stranger, C, 'purchased' property with notice of a negative covenant restricting the use of property, he would not be heard to say that he was now entitled to disregard the provisions of that covenant.[55] Such a principle would, naturally, have been subject to the overriding dictates of public policy which could adequately reflect any judicial distaste for particular restrictive conditions, such as price maintenance agreements. But this was not to be.

The Mareva Injunction

If the history of the injunction to enforce conditions restricting the use by strangers of personal property has been a disappointing one, the injunction has very recently proved a potent and novel means to restrain a defendant, who is alleged to be another's debtor, from taking assets out of the jurisdiction. 'You cannot get an injunction to restrain a man who is alleged to be a debtor from parting with his property.' These words of Cotton L.J. in *Lister* v. *Stubbs*[56] were, until recently, thought to state for English lawyers a principle of general application. But this appears no longer to be so, at least if the debtor is resident out of the jurisdiction but has assets within the jurisdiction which the plaintiff fears he might quickly remove on notice of the plaintiff's claim. It is only in the last four or five years that the English courts have been prepared to enjoin the alleged debtor in these circumstances. On a number of occasions the Court of Appeal[57] has said that the court has power to grant these injunctions; and the Commercial Bar, which conceived them, is most anxious that they should continue. So, in the only case to reach the House of Lords,[58] counsel who sought to discharge

55. The authorities are discussed by Scrutton J. in *L.C.C.* v. *Allan* [1914] 3 K.B. 642.
56. (1890) 45 Ch. D. 1,14.
57. *Nippon Yusen Kaisha* v. *Karageorgis* [1975] 1 W.L.R. 1093; *Mareva Compania Naviera S.A.* v. *International Bulk Carriers* [1975] 2 Lloyds Rep 509; *MBPXL Corpn.* v. *International Banking Corpn.* [1975] Court of Appeal Transcript 411; *Rasu Maritime S.A.* v. *Perusahaan Pertambangan Minjak Dan Gas Bumi Negara (Pertamina) and Government of Indonesia (as interveners)* [1978] Q.B. 644; *Cretanor Maritime Co. Ltd.* v. *Irish Management Ltd.* [1978] 1 W.L.R. 966; *The Assios* [1979] 1 Lloyds Rep 331; *Third Chandris Shipping Corpn.* v. *Unimarine S.A.* [1979] 2 All E.R. 972.
58. *The Siskina* [1977] 3 W.L.R. 818.

the injunction did so on grounds which did not directly question its propriety. Initially the *Mareva* injunction (which takes its name from one of the formative cases)[59] gave rise to as many questions as it answered. What sort of prima facie case must a plaintiff show, a strong one or simply an arguable one? What evidence must he adduce to demonstrate that the defendant might remove the assets from the jurisdiction? What evidence must the defendant give in order to obtain the discharge of the injunction? And, fundamentally, why should the courts treat a plaintiff whose defendant is out of the jurisdiction more favourably than a plaintiff whose defendant is within the jurisdiction? The answers to some of these, and other questions, are still far from clear.

The Origin of the Mareva Injunction

Debtors are tiresome creatures, and debtors who reside out of the jurisdiction are particularly tiresome. If the common law courts and the Court of Chancery did not recognise this, some customary courts did. For example, there existed in the great mercantile cities, such as London, Bristol, Exeter and Lancaster, a custom which was known as Foreign Attachment. 'The essence of its principle [was] to place an embargo on any property of the debtor, to ensure his appearance to answer the creditor's claim, and in default of such an appearance to take the property or part of it in satisfaction of the creditor's debt.'[60] But by the late nineteenth century this custom had fallen into desuetude, although it continued to flourish in the United States surviving attacks on its constitutionality.[61] The Mareva injunction is foreign attachment revived in all but name.

In two commercial cases, early in 1975,[62] the Court of Appeal granted an *ex parte* interlocutory injunction, pending the trial of the plaintiff's action, restraining a defendant resident out of the jurisdiction from disposing of assets within the jurisdiction. The background to these applications was the existence of one ship corporations registered abroad, charterers similarly incorporated, a depressed freight market, and the City of London where it was likely that the traceable assets of many such corporations could be found and where much international

59. *Mareva Compania Naviera S.A.* v. *International Bulk Carriers* [1975] 2 Lloyds Rep 509.
60. Woodthorpe Brandon, *A. Treatise upon the Customary Law of Foreign Attachment* (London, 1861), p.7.
61. *Pennoyer* v. *Ness*, 95 U.S. 714, 723-724, per Justice Field (1877). In France the procedure is known as *saisie conservatoire*.
62. See text accompanying notes 63 and 64 *post*.

arbitration takes place. So, in *Nippon Yusen Kaisha* v. *Karageorgis*[63], a ship owner sought an injunction against a charterer who, it was alleged, was in flagrant breach of the terms of the charter party. The ship owner deposed that, if the injunction were not granted, the charterer would remove money held to its account in an English bank. The court granted the injunction. Lord Denning M.R. said:[64]

> 'We are told that an injunction of this kind has never been done before. It has never been the practice of the English court to seize assets of a defendant in advance of judgement, or to restrain the disposal of them ... The time has come when we should revise our practice. There is no reason why the High Court or this court should not make an order such as is asked for here.'

Browne and Geoffrey Lane L.JJ. simply agreed with Lord Denning M.R.

In the second case, *Mareva Compania Naviera S.A.* v. *International Bulk Carriers S.A.*,[65] Lord Denning M.R. did not hesitate to grant the injunction on somewhat similar facts. But Roskill L.J. had considerable doubts about the High Court's jurisdiction to do so; in his experience, such an injunction had always been refused and it was only the very special facts of *Mareva* which persuaded him to concur with the Master of the Rolls.

In neither of these cases did the defendant appear or was he represented. Some months later, however, in *MPBXL Corpn.* v. *Intercontinental Banking Corpn.*[66] the grant of a *Mareva* injunction was successfully opposed. The Court of Appeal described the injunction as an 'exceptional remedy', which should only be granted on clear evidence that the defendant had assets within the jurisdiction and where the plaintiff's claim was not disputed or seriously disputed.[67] The effect of that decision was to put something of a brake on applications for Mareva injunctions. It was not until 1977, in the *Pertamina*[68] case, that the High Court's jurisdiction to grant these injunctions was confirmed and indeed significantly enlarged. In *Pertamina* the Court of Appeal refused to exercise its discretion to grant an injunction for there was some doubt whether the assets which were to be the subject matter of the injunction belonged to the defendant. But it did not doubt that it would be 'just and convenient' to do so in an appropriate case. For a foreign defendant was in a significantly different position from a defen-

63. [1975] 1 W.L.R. 1093.
64. At pp. 1094-1095.
65. [1975] 2 Lloyds Rep 509.
66. Unreported; [1975] Court of Appeal Transcript 411.
67. Cited in *Third Chandris Shipping Corpn.* v. *Unimarine S.A.* [1979] 2 All E.R. 972, 975, *per* Mustill J.
68. [1978] Q.B. 644.

dant resident within jurisdiction. As Kerr J. said at first instance in *Pertamina*: [69]

> 'A plaintiff has what appears to be an indisputable claim against the defendant outside the jurisdiction, but with assets within the jurisdiction which he could easily remove, and which the court is satisfied are liable to be removed unless an injunction is granted. The plaintiff is then in the following difficulty. First, he needs leave to serve the defendant outside the jurisdiction, and the defendant is then given time to enter an appearance from the date when he is served, all of which takes several weeks or even months. Secondly, it is only then that the plaintiff can apply for summary judgement under R.S.C. Ord. XIV with a view to levying execution on the defendant's assets here. Thirdly, however, on being apprised of these proceedings, the defendant is liable to remove his assets, thereby precluding the plaintiff in advance from enjoying the fruits of a judgement which appears irrestible on the evidence before the court. The defendant can then largely ignore the plaintiff's claim in the courts of this country and snap his fingers at any judgement which may be given against him.'

The principles established in *Pertamina* and refined in subsequent cases 'gave a new dimension to the Mareva injunction.'[70] Thereafter it was not an exceptional remedy; it became common place. 'At present, applications are being made at the rate of twenty per month. Almost all are granted'. [71]

The Principles Underlying the Grant of the Mareva Injunction

After *Pertamina* there have been three significant decisions: One is that of the House of Lords in *The Siskina*, [72] and there are two of the Court of Appeal, *Cretanor Maritime Co. Ltd.* v. *Irish Maritime Management Ltd.* [73] and *Third Chandris Shipping Corporation* v. *Unimarine S.A.* [74] From them the following propositions may be gleaned:

1. The jurisdiction of the High Court to grant an injunction rests on Section 45 of the Supreme Court of Judicature (Consolidation) Act 1925 which gives the High Court power to 'grant a mandamus or injunction or appoint a receiver by an interlocutory order in all cases which it appears to the court to be just or convenient so to do'.

69. Cited in [1978] Q.B. 644, 660-661.
70. *Third Chandris Shipping Corpn.* v. *Unimarine S.A.* [1979] 2 All E.R. 972, 976, *per* Mustill J.
71. See note 70.
72. [1977] 3 W.L.R. 818.
73. [1978] 1 W.L.R. 966.
74. [1979] 2 All E.R. 972.

2. The effectiveness of the application depends on it being made *ex parte*; otherwise the defendant would have the opportunity of removing the assets out of the jurisdiction. [75] But because the application is made *ex parte*, the defendant or his agent should be informed immediately that it has issued and he should be told that he is at liberty to have the injunction discharged at any time by notice. [76] Moreover the plaintiff should make 'full and frank disclosure of all matters in his knowledge:', and should give particulars of his claim against the defendant. [77] He must also give an undertaking to pay damages in the event that his substantive claim fails.

3. The plaintiff should give 'some grounds for believing that the defendants have assets here' [78]. At one time it was thought that the *Mareva* injunction could only restrain the defendant from removing assets described and identified by the plaintiff in his affidavit. [79] But in practice the form of the *Mareva* order was always wider, to restrain the defendant 'from removing or taking any steps to remove *any assets* from within the jurisdiction of this court or otherwise disposing of the same' and, in particular, the assets specifically identified in the affidavit. [80] The Court of Appeal has now affirmed that it is enough that it is deposed that prima facie assets exist and where they may be found. [81] 'In most cases the plaintiff will not know the extent of the assets. He will only have indications of them.' [82] So, the injunction may relate wholly or in part to a body of unspecified but ascertainable assets which might increase or decrease during the life of the injunction. [83]

4. In most cases the plaintiff has sought to arrest money in a bank account. Indeed it appears to be enough that the defendant has a bank account within the jurisdiction even though the bank account may be overdrawn. [84]

It lies against goods, although it has been said that the injunction should not readily be granted if the goods are part of the defendant's stock in trade and which could, if frozen by the injunction, bring the trade to a standstill. In *Rena K.* [85] where the defendant sought unsuc-

75. See text accompanying footnote 69.
76. *The Assios* [1979] 1 Lloyds Rep 331.
77. *Third Chandris Shipping Corpn.* v. *Unimarine S.A.* [1979] 2 All E.R. 972, 984, *per* Lord Denning M.R., citing *The Assios* [1979] 1 Lloyds Rep 331.
78. *Ante* n. 77.
79. *MPBXL Corpn.* v. *Intercontinental Banking Corpn.* [1975] Court of Appeal Transcript 411.
80. See *Cretanor Maritime Co. Ltd.* v. *Irish Marine Management Ltd.* [1978] 1 W.L.R. 966, 972.
81. *Ante* n. 77.
82. *Ante* n. 77
83. *Cretanor Maritime Co. Ltd.* v. *Irish Management Ltd.* [1978] 1 W.L.R. 966.
84. *Third Chandris Shipping Corpn.* v. *Unimarine S.A.* [1979] 2 All E.R. 972, 985, *per* Lord Denning M.R., 988, *per* Lawton and Cumming-Bruce L.JJ.
85. [1979] 1 All E.R. 398. These observations were obiter.

cessfully to resist the injunction on that ground, Brandon J. exercised the benefit of hindsight to conclude that, after the asset, a ship, had been released, the defendant ship owners had laid her up and had not attempted to use her as part of their trade.

It will be recalled that the *Mareva* injunction was originally only granted if the plaintiff's claim was not 'seriously disputed'.[86] In other words, one had to show a case so strong that, if the defendant was resident within jurisdiction, summary judgement would be given against him. In *Pertamina*, Lord Denning M.R. refused to limit the discretion of the court to cases 'so plain that the plaintiff can get judgement under R.S.C. Ord. XIV'.[87] Replying on the authority of the *House of Lords in American Cyanamid Co.* v. *Ethicon Ltd.*,[88] he concluded that it would be enough that the plaintiff could show that he had 'a good arguable case', that an award of damages would be an ineffective remedy, and that balance of justice and convenience demanded the grant of the injunction. In the court below Kerr J. had refused the injunction because the plaintiff's case was not strong enough to have persuaded him to grant summary judgement if the defendant had been within jurisdiction; and the other member of the Court of Appeal, Orr L.J., also seemed to think that the court should take into account the apparent strength or weakness of the plaintiff's case.[89]

However it would appear from *Third Chandris*[90] that Lord Denning's view presently prevails, even though this is the only occasion upon which the Master of the Rolls has enthusiastically followed the principles established by House of Lords in *American Cyanamid.*[91]

5. What evidence must the plaintiff adduce to demonstrate that it is likely that the defendant would remove assets from the jurisdiction before any judgement or award is satisfied? In *Third Chandris,*[92] Mustill J. answered the question in this way: 'Prima facie by demonstrating that the asset is present, that it is movable and that the defendant is abroad.' He accepted that 'some adverse inference' would have to be drawn from the mere fact that the defendant is abroad if the *Mareva* jurisdiction is to survive let alone flourish. The Court of Appeal refused to go this far. Lord Denning M.R., Lawton L.J. and Cumming-Bruce L.J. all agreed that 'the mere fact that the defendant is abroad is not by itself sufficient'.[93] Lord Denning and Cumming-Bruce L.J. gave very

86. See text accompanying footnote 67.
87. [1978] Q.B. 644, 661.
88. [1975] A.C. 396.
89. [1978] Q.B. 644, 664. See also *Cretanor Maritime Co. Ltd.* v. *Irish Management Ltd.* [1978] 1 W.L.R. 966, 975, *per* Buckley L.J.
90. [1979] 2 All E.R. 972.
91. [1975] A.C. 396.
92. [1979] 2 All E.R. 972, 977.
93. [1979] 2 All E.R. 972, 985, 987, 988.

little guidance as to the quality of evidence which would satisfy the court; no 'reputable foreign company' should 'be plagued with a *Mareva* injunction simply because it has agreed to London arbitration'. [94]

Lawton L.J. was more specific. In his view, 'an affidavit ... should give enough particulars of the plaintiff's case to enable the court to assess its strength and should set out what enquiries have been made about the defendants' business and what information has been revealed, including that relating to its size, origins, business domicile, the location of its known assets and the circumstances in which the dispute has arisen'. [95]

6. The converse to the previous question is this: what must the defendant do to secure the discharge of the injunction? In *Third Chandris* the defendant corporations failed, even though their affidavit stated that they were substantial corporations with about one hundred ships on charter, that they had a good defence to the ship owners' claims, and that they could honour any judgement against them. However, they did not give any details of their financial position; there was no balance sheet or statement of account and no evidence was given by any director or officer of the company. A defendant must produce 'solid evidence', and the defendant corporations had failed to do so. [96] Moreover the Court of Appeal was not deterred by the threat that, if the injunction were granted, the defendant corporations would move their business away from London.

7. In *The Siskina,* [97] The House of Lords refused to enjoin a defendant from dealing with the proceeds of an insurance claim which were payable to him in London, in circumstances where the English courts had no jurisdiction whatsoever over the plaintiff's substantive claim. 'In order to obtain a *Mareva* injunction there has to be in existence a substantive cause of action on which the plaintiff is suing or about to sue in the High Court in England or is enforcing or about to enforce by arbitration in England.' [98] The dispute between the cargo owners and the ship owner was not justifiable in England for the bills of lading were governed by Italian law and the cargo was arrested *in rem* in Cyprus.

8. In *Cretanor Maritime Co. Ltd.* v. *Irish Maritime Management Ltd.,* [99] the Court of Appeal allowed the debenture holder of the alleged debtor to apply for the discharge of a *Mareva* injunction which had been obtained by the plaintiff. The *Mareva* injunction was not an attachment in the sense that it enabled the plaintiff to seize the defen-

94. [1979] 2 All E.R. 972, 987.
95. [1979] 2 All E.R. 972, 987.
96. [1979] 2 All E.R. 972, 985, 987-8.
97. [1977] 3 W.L.R. 818.
98. *Third Chandris Shipping Corpn.* v. *Unimarine S.A.* [1979] 2 All E.R. 972, 983, *per* Lord Denning M.R.
99. [1978] 1 W.L.R. 966. Cf. now *Iraqi Ministry of Defence* v. *Arcepey Shipping Co. S.A.* [1980] 1 All E.R. 480.

dants' assets under some writ or like command. The *Mareva* injunction was, simply, 'relief in personam'.[100] 'It does not affect the seizure of any assets. It merely restrains the owner from dealing with the asset in certain ways.'[101] The court refused, therefore, to allow the plaintiff through a *Mareva* injunction to obtain indirectly the position of a secured creditor.

The Unresolved Questions

At first the *Mareva* injunction was regarded as a very special exception to the principle that you cannot restrain a person whom you allege to be your debtor from removing assets out of the jurisdiction. In *Pertamina,* Kerr J. attempted to justify its existence on the ground that a plaintiff's claim could otherwise be easily frustrated by the defendant quickly removing assets from the jurisdiction.[102] But a plaintiff may be equally vulnerable to the wiles of a resident defendant who is able to persuade the court to give him leave to defend. It was these considerations which led Lord Hailsham in *The Siskina*[103] to say that sooner or later the courts or the legislature would have to choose between two alternatives: either 'the position of the plaintiff making the claim against an English based defendant would have to be altered or the principle of the *Mareva* cases will have to be modified'.

Lord Denning M.R. would not hesitate to extend the *Mareva* injunction to restrain even a defendant resident within the jurisdiction from disposing of his assets so as to defeat a plaintiff's claim before judgement.[104] And in *Third Chandris*[105] he has said that the Court of Appeal has already done so, in the then unreported case of *Chartered Bank* v. *Daklouche*.[106] If this is so, then the *Mareva* injunction will no longer be an exceptional remedy, and the principle of Cotton L.J. in *Lister* v. *Stubbs*[107] will be overthrown.

There is some force in the argument, particularly since England's entry into the E.E.C., that it is not tenable to apply different principles to govern the attachment of assets, depending upon whether the assets belong to a national who is normally resident within jurisdiction or to a foreigner who is normally resident out of the jurisdiction.[108] But it is

100. [1978] 1 W.L.R. 966, 974, *per* Buckley L.J.
101. *Ante* n. 100; as did the old procedure of foreign attachment.
102. See text accompanying footnote 69.
103. [1978] 3 W.L.R. 818, 830.
104. There are hints in *Pertamina* [1978] Q.B. 644.
105. [1979] 2 All E.R. 972, 983-984.
106. March 16, 1979. It is now reported in: [1980] 1 All E.R. 205. Contrast *The Agrabele* [1979] 2 Lloyd's Rep 112.
107. (1890) 45 Ch. D. 1, 14; *Ante* p. 61.
108. See Sir Michael Kerr's remarks in (1978) 41 M.L.R. 1, 14-15.

doubtful whether it would be wise to accept *Chartered Bank* v. *Daklouche*. The implications of any change would be profound, and would blur even further the boundaries between property and contract. A plaintiff has always been able to restrain a defendant whom he says is his trustee from disposing of assets which are alleged to belong to the trust. It is an entirely different question whether a defendant who is alleged to be a debtor should be similarly restrained from dealing freely with his *own* assets, particularly if the plaintiff has merely to show that he has an arguable case. At a minimum, there surely is something to be said for the reaffirmation of the principle that a plaintiff can obtain a *Mareva* injunction only if he demonstrates that he has so strong a case that he would obtain summary judgment if the defendant had been within the jurisdiction.

It is predictable that great commercial inconvenience may be caused by the grant of a *Mareva* injunction ex parte. In *Third Chandris* [109] Mustill J. accepted this but did not consider it to be conclusive. He said:

> 'The whole point of *Mareva* jurisdiction is that the plaintiff proceeds by stealth, so as to pre-empt any action by the defendant to remove his assets from the jurisdiction. This entails that the defendant finds that his bank account has been blocked before he has any idea of what is going to happen. This may have extremely serious consequences. Cheques or bills drawn on the account may be presented at a time when adequate funds are available to meet them, and may yet be dishonoured because the injunction inhibits the bank in making payment. Moreover the very secrecy of the procedure deprives a defendant of the opportunity to make a timely alternative arrangement for presentment or payment abroad. The dishonour of the defendant's paper may have disastrous consequences; and all this in a situation where the plaintiff had shown no more than an arguable case. An undertaking by the plaintiff for damages may not always be a sufficient indemnity for the loss the defendant may suffer. Again the blocking of an account may have very serious consequences for a defendant who is dependent on cash flow for his commercial survival. The case of a charterer provides an example. On a rising market the free use of his bank account is a crucial importance. The non-payment of hire may lead to the loss of a charter. It is of no consolation to say that he can apply to have the ex parte injunction discharged, if by the time his application is heard the damage may have been done.'

Nonetheless, the judge found that 'the considerations the other way', in particular the fact that the number of applications to discharge *Mareva* injunctions 'is remarkably small', indicated that these potential hard-

109. [1979] 2 All E.R. 972, 978.

ships have not in fact materialised. But arguments based upon negative inferences are dangerous arguments. For example, as the judge admitted, the injunctions may have been voluntarily lifted because of the readiness of the defendants to provide financial guarantees rather than to have recourse to the courts. In *Cretanor Maritime,*[110] the Court of Appeal rejected an attempt to manipulate the *Mareva* injunction so as to elevate the plaintiff into a position of a secured creditor. The court properly emphasised that the relief was a relief *in personam.* 'It does not affect a seizure of any asset. It merely restrains the owner from dealing with the asset in certain ways ... All that the injunction achieves is in truth to prohibit the owner from doing certain things in relation to the asset'.[111] Yet if it is the case that an injunction may in practice be lifted only if the defendant provides security for the plaintiff's claim, that security may give the plaintiff a real preference if there is a foreign bankruptcy. In *Pertamina,*[112] Lord Denning viewed this with equanimity. But in *Cretanor Maritime,*[113] Buckley L.J. thought that it was a matter for debate whether 'it is justifiable for the court to lend its authority in the exercise of a discretionary jurisdiction and one based fundamentally on equitable principles to bringing pressure to bear on a party in this way ...' I share the Lord Justice's hesitations. The form of the injunction, referring to a body of unspecified assets which might increase during the term of the injunction and which might include money or goods of the defendant's stock in trade, in itself brings very considerable pressure to bear on any defendant.

Hitherto the *Mareva* injunction has been confined to commercial disputes. But there is no reason in principle to think that it should continue to be confined, in Lord Hailsham's felicitous phrase, to the 'Arcadia of the commercial list.'[114] For example, it could be a powerful weapon in disputes between estranged husbands and wives, particularly if the *Mareva* injunction is extended so as to reach defendants within the jurisdiction. There are indications that the courts are now realising some of the dangers of a promiscuous extension of *Mareva* injunctions. Lord Denning on more than one occasion has said 'that we must be careful that it is not stretched too far, else we should be endangering it. It must be kept for proper circumstances and not extended so far as to endanger the proper conduct of business.'[115]

The House of Lords has still to bless the jurisdiction to grant *Mareva*

110. [1978] 1 W.L.R. 966.
111. [1978] 1 W.L.R. 966, 974, *per* Buckley L.J.
112. [1978] Q.B. 644, 662.
113. [1978] 1 W.L.R. 966, 974-975.
114. [1978] 3 W.L.R. 818, 830.
115. *The Assios* [1970] 1 Lloyds Rep 331, 334. See also *Third Chandris Shipping Corpn.* v. *Unimarine S.A.* [1979].

injunctions. Lord Denning has attempted to pre-empt their option by saying that 'if the House had any doubts about our jurisdiction in the matter I should have expected them [in *The Siskina*] to give voice to them, rather than let the legal profession continue in error.'[116] *Mareva* injunctions have now flourished for some years; and neither the legal profession nor the users of the commercial court will be anxious to kill the goose that lays the golden egg. They are now probably too firmly established to be overthrown. But the years that lie ahead may well see a restriction of the ambit and scope of the injunction rather than a further period of expansion. In my view, it should be sparingly exercised. In particular:

a. The *Mareva* injunction should not be extended to attach the assets of defendants within the jurisdiction;

b. the plaintiff should be required to adduce evidence to show that his claim is so strong that it is not seriously disputed; and that the defendant is likely to remove assets from the jurisdiction;[117]

c. the *Mareva* injunction should not be used to circumvent indirectly any statutory provision.[118]

116. [1979] 2 All E.R. 972, 983.
117. See now, *Monleachi* v. *Shinco (U.K.) Ltd.* [1979], W.L.R. 1180.
118. This was done in *Rena K* [1979] 1 All E.R. 397.